200+
Proven Strategies
for
Teaching
Reading GRADES K–8

KATHY PEREZ

Solution Tree | Press

a division of
Solution Tree

555 North Morton Street
Bloomington, IN 47404
800.733.6786 (toll free) / 812.336.7700
FAX: 812.336.7790

email: info@SolutionTree.com
SolutionTree.com

Visit **go.SolutionTree.com/literacy** to download the free reproducibles in this book.

Printed in the United States of America

20 19 18 17 16   1 2 3 4 5

FSC
www.fsc.org
MIX
Paper from
responsible sources
FSC® C011935

Library of Congress Control Number: 2016952633

Solution Tree
Jeffrey C. Jones, CEO
Edmund M. Ackerman, President

Solution Tree Press
President: Douglas M. Rife
Editorial Director: Tonya Maddox Cupp
Managing Production Editor: Caroline Weiss
Senior Production Editor: Suzanne Kraszewski
Senior Editor: Amy Rubenstein
Copy Chief: Sarah Payne-Mills
Proofreader: Jessi Finn
Text and Cover Designer: Laura Cox
Editorial Assistants: Jessi Finn and Kendra Slayton

Acknowledgments

Solution Tree Press would like to thank the following reviewers:

Christy Banks
  Reading Specialist
  Liberty Elementary School
  South Riding, Virginia

Jeanette Brosam
  Instructional Coach
  Franklin Middle School
  Champaign, Illinois

Elaine Delgado
  Reading/Dyslexia Interventionist
  Jack C. Binion Elementary School
  Richland Hills, Texas

Samantha Harris
  Reading Recovery® Teacher Leader
  Alpine School District
  American Fork, Utah

Patti James
  Literacy Coach
  Palm Bay Magnet High School
  Melbourne, Florida

Tara Looney
  Title I Reading Teacher
  Concordia Elementary School
  Concordia, Missouri

Natalie McAvoy
  Reading Specialist/Interventionist/
    Coach
  Tibbets Elementary School
  Elkhorn, Wisconsin

Peggy Miller
  Reading Interventionist
  Timber Creek Elementary School
  Raymore, Missouri

Cindi Rigsbee
  Regional Education Facilitator
  North Carolina Teacher of the Year
    2009
  Gravelly Hill Middle School
  Efland, North Carolina

Melanie Sims
   Literacy Coach
   Highland Park Elementary School
   Bloomington, Indiana

Frances W. Stewart
   Literacy Coach, Department of
      Curriculum and Instruction
   Monroe County Community School
      Corporation
   Bloomington, Indiana

Kris Stewart
   Literacy Coach/IB Coordinator
   Childs Elementary School
   Bloomington, Indiana

Visit **go.SolutionTree.com/literacy**
to download the free reproducibles in this book.

Table of Contents

About the Author

**Kathy Perez, EdD,** an award-winning classroom teacher, administrator, and author, has worked with students from preschool to postcollege. Kathy is currently a professor of education at Saint Mary's College of California, director of teaching leadership, and coordinator of professional development and outreach.

An "education evangelist," Kathy is an acclaimed international educational consultant and motivational speaker specializing in instructional strategies and creative approaches to literacy, learning, and leadership development. She integrates state-of-the-art methods and research with passion and practical insights from her own classroom experiences.

Kathy has extensive teaching experience as a general educator, special educator, literacy coach, and curriculum and staff development coordinator. She has worked extensively with teachers, administrators, and parents throughout the United States, Canada, Europe, Qatar, the Caribbean, Africa, New Zealand, Brazil, Australia, Thailand, Colombia, Hong Kong, and Singapore. Her best-selling books include *More Than 100 Brain-Friendly Tools and Strategies for Literacy Instruction*, *The Co-Teaching Book of Lists*, and her latest book, *The New Inclusion: Differentiated Strategies to Engage ALL Students*.

To learn more about Kathy Perez and her work, visit http://drkathyperez.com and follow her on Twitter @DrKathyPerez.

To book Kathy Perez for professional development, contact pd@SolutionTree.com.

Introduction

The purpose of this book is to provide practical, research-based techniques and interventions to help readers achieve success in literacy—particularly with struggling readers. Nothing motivates students to read like knowing how to read! In my many years of experience as a classroom teacher, literacy coach, and special education teacher, I have found that often teachers in general education classrooms don't feel prepared to teach students who need additional support. Struggling readers need more than whole-class instruction in discrete skills that don't transfer to real reading and life skills. Learning to read is critical to students' academic success and has a tremendous impact on their social and emotional development and their achievements, yet little consideration is given to helping teachers learn how struggling students become proficient readers.

Reading specialists and literacy coaches assist classroom educators in many schools; however, classroom teachers still need to develop techniques to support those who struggle with the literacy process, especially with the implementation of Common Core State Standards. The standards represent a significant shift from previous standards, and there is a lack of specificity regarding implementation. The standards alone can't overcome the learning challenges many students face; teachers need practical intervention strategies they can integrate into any lesson to meet the unique needs of diverse learners. This book provides educators with a range of engaging and effective techniques to increase instructional impact for all students in the classroom.

Teachers need to learn how to design and implement effective literacy lessons that use brain-based research to maximize learning. Student engagement during literacy instruction has a profound impact on what students learn (Yoncheva, Wise, & McCandliss et al., 2015). The strategies in this book will support students' individual learning styles and their cognitive and emotional needs and development.

This book is unique. It goes beyond individual teacher assistance and provides creative systems that work with a student's literacy education to support the needs of readers. The strategies and routines featured in this book are flexible for small-group work and adaptable to whole-class or individualized intervention.

I hope to encourage and nourish the continuous growth of professional educators with this book. Teachers will have the tools to determine what works with struggling readers and all students. They can use that information to go beyond the specific strategies this book describes to create their own brain-based strategies for exceptional learners.

The Knowledge Base: What Does the Research Say?

Literacy is the key to success in school and throughout life. When I started in the profession, I was told, "All teachers are teachers of reading." This is a challenging assumption (Brozo & Simpson, 2007; Ivey & Fisher, 2006). During my career, I have broadened my thinking about literacy success to include reading, writing, speaking, listening, thinking, and communicating—all ways that humans learn. Teachers need to use strategies to engage learners in all literacy processes. This represents a significant conceptual shift from simply "teaching reading."

In addition, schools traditionally assume that cognitive and academic achievements are distinct from emotion. School mission statements often express respect for individual differences and sensitivity to students' culturally and linguistically diverse backgrounds; however, that mission does not always translate into practice to celebrate unique learning styles. Rather than focusing on individual differences and student talents, curriculum plans are usually based on learning specified content and developing specific skills aimed at meeting distinct standards—an approach that has gained momentum, has informed educational policy, and set the national educational agenda in the 2000s.

Traditionally, teachers haven't been empowered with high-quality strategies to equip them with the sophisticated range of skills and curriculum formats necessary in an inclusive classroom. However, research points to the importance of differentiated instruction (Chapman & Gregory, 2013; Tomlinson, 2014) and cooperative, flexible grouping. It also stresses research-based conclusions on reading comprehension. This research includes integration and application of the work of P. David Pearson (2003) and Richard Allington (2012) about what works with struggling readers.

As educators in inclusive classrooms, we want to support struggling readers while not letting our focus on their learning differences diminish the quality of teaching for the rest of the class. Fortunately, brain research (Jensen, 2008; Wolfe, 2001) confirms that strategies benefiting learners with special challenges are appropriate for engaging all learners. Teachers need to use a variety of strategies and techniques to engage students' brains to make meaning out of what they read to optimize learning

(Caine, 2000). Understanding this brain learning research will increase educators' confidence and competence with the methods that are most compatible with how students acquire, retain, and use information to become more literate.

The Nature of Content: What Is It About?

The strategies in this book are firmly rooted in research and are very practical for struggling readers and all learners. When teachers use and adapt these strategies to meet their students' diverse needs, they will also reach the learners at the extremes of the continuum and prevent students from falling through the cracks.

The core ideas in this book include:

- ★ The most successful instructional strategies are those that teach for meaning and understanding.
- ★ The most productive and learning-conducive classrooms are student-centered yet high in reasonable challenge.
- ★ Actively engaged and motivated students will strive to meet meaningful goals and standards.

The Primary Audience for This Book

Educators in elementary and middle school classrooms will find this book particularly helpful. Students acquiring English will also find success with these engaging strategies. The book is designed to be a reference for teachers to access new ideas and interventions that breathe new life into their literacy lessons. The strategies are effective tools for a broad range of ages and ability levels. Teachers may need to adapt and adjust the materials based on student needs.

This book is also appropriate for professional development and teacher book clubs and can be a resource for reading specialists and literacy coaches. Literacy educators and teacher educators will find this book a useful resource for their preservice and graduate classes.

Experienced teachers, beginning teachers, literacy coaches, special educators, and preservice teachers will find this book translates sound and relevant theory into practical classroom applications.

Text Tour: A Roadmap of Chapters and Content

Chapter 1 looks at the traits of good readers and struggling readers. It examines who struggles with reading, how to identify a struggling reader, and the early signs of reading difficulty.

Chapter 2 looks at the components of effective programs. It identifies the key elements, how educators develop strategic readers, what factors impact reading comprehension, and the power of intervention. It reveals step-by-step support strategies for struggling readers.

Chapter 3 examines early literacy intervention. It shows how we identify problems and monitor progress, find classroom-based assessment practices, and use flexible grouping and organization. It explores the supports we can provide for emergent reading and writing.

Chapter 4 examines vocabulary strategies, including vocabulary acquisition and use, promoting word consciousness, providing rich language experiences, and strategies for discovering the wonder of words.

Chapter 5 looks at graphic organizers and how they help students understand critical concepts, ideas, and relationships in what they read as well as how they can help students organize their thinking.

Chapter 6 looks at content strategies for navigating informational text by sharing techniques and strategies for student success.

Chapter 7 explores questioning techniques for higher-level thinking. It examines why asking questions is important and techniques for student engagement, redirecting, probing, responding, and differentiating.

Chapter 8 discusses developing an action plan for success. Where do you begin when organizing and managing your literacy classroom?

The appendix provides a toolbox of easy-to-implement strategies for a multifaceted approach to teaching literacy.

Final Thoughts

This book is dedicated to you, the educator. I am honored you have selected it as part of your professional library. I hope you use the tools within these pages—the plethora of possibilities—to instill a can-do spirit that helps propel your students from struggling to succeeding. You have the power to make *the* difference in your students' lives today and every day. As a teacher of reading, you hold the key to students' success in your hands.

1

The Struggling Reader

What comes to mind when you hear the term *struggling reader*? Does it bring to mind specific descriptors, such as *slow*, *frustrated*, or *unmotivated*? To struggle as a reader means to cope with an inability to perform well. Quite simply, struggling readers lack the essential literacy skills of proficient readers. But what does that mean in practice? The term *struggling reader* often implies a single category defined by a single problem. In reality, however, a wide range of reading problems are identified in school. Some struggling students can't read the text. Others might have difficulty comprehending the meaning of what they read. Still others are just not interested in what they are reading. Students might read below grade level or be challenged with phonics, fluency, or vocabulary. No two struggling readers will have identical profiles.

Struggling readers have not developed a reading system that allows them to construct meaning. They have often felt defeated, which has contributed to a negative attitude that has turned off their desire to read. Many have adopted an attitude of learned helplessness and may exhibit inappropriate behaviors to mask their inability to read and comprehend. However, struggling is not the same as failing. Narrow definitions are limiting to students rather than helpful. According to the International Reading Association and the National Council of Teachers of English (2010), all students "have a right to instruction designed with their specific needs in mind."

Let's look at what it means to be a struggling reader. These students often do not understand the purposes of reading and the skills necessary for success: fluency, inflection, and expression. Some students have had limited exposure to literature or Standard English vocabulary in the home. Many at-risk readers do not have adequate background knowledge to develop appropriate schema.

Students with poor visual processing skills might have difficulty with visual tracking, hand-eye coordination, visual figure-ground discrimination, double vision, and the ability to communicate clearly what they see or don't see. Students with learning disabilities might have difficulty with processing and memorizing information. Some will learn words in one context and not transfer them to the next.

It is important to understand the different ways that students learn and to provide them with diverse opportunities for learning throughout the day.

Causes of Reading Comprehension Failure

The ultimate goal in reading instruction is for students to become sufficiently fluent to understand what they read. Reading comprehension is a highly complex cognitive process that relies on several components if students are to be successful. It depends on understanding spoken language and development of the meaning-making process. These are of paramount importance if students are to interact successfully with a text. Focusing on the causes of reading comprehension failure helps educators better understand the profile of the struggling reader. These causes include:

- ★ Lack of effective comprehension strategies
- ★ Vocabulary deficits
- ★ Inadequate background knowledge on the topic
- ★ Deficient word recognition skills
- ★ Lack of awareness of the different writing conventions the author uses (text features, humor, expressions, and dialogue, for example)
- ★ Poor ability to remember or recall verbal information (word storage and retrieval)
- ★ Inadequate verbal reasoning (the ability to "read between the lines"; Lyon, 1999)

Research tells us that readers who comprehend well are usually good decoders (Allington, 2012; International Reading Association & National Council of Teachers of English, 2010). In addition, proficient readers recognize when they do not understand and shift their use of strategies as needed to increase their understanding. Teaching students to use comprehension strategies every time they read is key. Educators must encourage students to visualize settings and characters or processes being explained as they read.

What to Look For

Carefully observe and identify struggling readers at an early age to assess their progress, and design appropriate instruction to meet their needs. Some may experience just one reading issue, and others may manifest multiple symptoms of struggle that interfere with the reading process. Teachers can look for some warning signals. Diagnosing the root cause or causes of the struggle begins with identifying certain qualities and characteristics of weak reading. Some of the more common characteristics observed in students who are struggling with reading include they:

★ Do not see the value or benefit of being able to read
★ Lack accuracy in sounding out words
★ Guess more without using context clues
★ Give up easily and become frustrated more quickly than other students
★ Use word-by-word reading that lacks fluency, unless text is read from memory or has been carefully rehearsed
★ Exhibit word and letter reversals and omissions frequently
★ Are very reluctant to participate in read-aloud activities
★ May have a lower sense of self-esteem and confidence level
★ Lack simple strategies for decoding and comprehension when attempting to read that good readers use
★ Try to avoid reading and often hide that they can't read
★ Have a negative attitude toward reading and make excuses not to read
★ May have tracking problems and skip words or misread words due to eye sweep movements

These characteristics are most frequently observed in struggling students; however, the list is certainly not exhaustive and does not include all the characteristics or warning signs that you might observe in your classroom. Each student is unique with his or her own entry point to learning. For example, you might have students who have an inability to manipulate individual speech sounds in words—that is, they lack phonological awareness. Other students might have difficulty with visual naming speed. Some students are unable to chunk words or sentences into smaller parts or do not have good reading-to-learn strategies. Some students do not use what they do know. In other words, the students do not know specific compensatory techniques to overcome their difficulties and utilize their strengths.

Why Struggling Students Don't Read, Aren't Motivated, or Are Reluctant to Read

By the time struggling students reach high school, they may equate reading with ridicule, failure, or exclusively school-related tasks. The reasons they don't read are as diverse as the students themselves. The key is how to identify and properly address their unique needs. Have you heard a student say, "I hate to read"? What does it mean, why did he or she say it, and what can you do about it? The following are common factors among reluctant readers.

★ Reading is "not cool" within their social group.
★ Many struggling students have attention-deficit disorder and are unable to sit and focus on content for long periods.
★ Many students experience stress from both home and school to achieve more in reading, which fosters their avoidance.

★ Some may consider reading as a solitary act but thrive in groups.

★ Some adolescents view reading as a part of the adult world that does not concern them.

★ Many struggling readers grow up in illiterate households. There may be a lack of reading role models and a lack of access to books.

★ Reluctant readers who have faced years of frustration may equate reading with failure and see it as only a school-related task.

★ Reading is perceived as a very static form of information compared to television and the Internet.

★ Students are not very motivated or excited about ideas. They prefer to experience life directly, not vicariously through words.

★ Students who struggle with literacy often become self-absorbed and preoccupied with their immediate needs and have difficulty seeing the relevance between books and their lives.

Many struggling readers are anxious about school. They may appear to be unmotivated because they lack confidence in their ability to read (Kos, 1991). They may attribute their challenges with reading to the difficulty of the text, distractions, vision problems, or unfair teacher expectations. Many deny that their own lack of skill as a reader is at the core of the problem. Some give up on the process entirely, adopting a sense of learned helplessness. Teachers often perceive this lack of participation in classroom activities as defiance or a lack of motivation.

Two variables strongly affect motivation: (1) whether we expect to be successful at a task and (2) how much value we place on that success (Wigfield, 2000). Students generally believe they are successful because of ability, effort, or just luck. However, struggling students find that school is not a supportive place to be. Robert Marzano and his colleagues (Marzano, Pickering, & Pollock, 2001) find that successful individuals believe they can succeed because of ability and fail due to lack of effort. In contrast, unmotivated individuals tend to perceive success as luck and failure as a lack of ability (Weiner, 1979). Unmotivated individuals play the role of victim very well.

Because of this and after a series of failures, some students believe that they are not capable of success and tend to give up without even trying. Teachers need to continuously scaffold instruction for success. Reinforcing the connection between effort and achievement with students at risk of reading failure is important. Creating a success-oriented environment in the classroom and instilling in the students a "can-do" spirit by setting attainable goals can have a profound, positive effect on struggling students (Marzano et al., 2001).

Furthermore, struggling students who have experienced many years of frustration and failure are hesitant to read aloud in front of their peers. These students may check out of the reading process and become reluctant readers because they may be repeatedly presented with material that does not interest them or seem relevant to them. As teachers, our challenge is to show these students how their work is meaningful and help them become self-motivated by demonstrating how reading can be a bridge to learning things that do matter to them. The strategies presented in this book go beyond just "covering material"—rather, they provide teachers with opportunities to uncover content for students by using motivating and meaningful methods.

What Good Readers Do

Now let's focus on the skills and traits of good readers and the strategies they use. The traits of good readers provide instructional targets to strive for in your lessons (National Reading Panel, 2000). Good readers:

★ Look for meaning in words that they read
★ Pay attention to the author's voice and craft
★ Ask questions as they read and keep reading to find answers
★ Evaluate what they read
★ Make predictions about what will happen next
★ Self-correct if the text doesn't make sense
★ Bring their background knowledge and experience of subject matter to the text
★ Know how to visualize as they read
★ Are fluent and understand the flow of language and sounds of letters and shapes of words
★ Experience reading as a holistic process and proceed with automaticity in the meaning-making process
★ Know how to infer and "read between the lines"
★ Understand what they read, reread, and find answers to their questions and predictions as they read
★ Talk about the book, stories, or text with others and make connections
★ Use context clues for the meaning of challenging vocabulary words
★ Are aware of text structure and evaluate what they read
★ Read with a purpose, comprehending as they go
★ Constantly check their comprehension to be sure they understand and pay attention to the task of reading
★ Infer the author's attitude and voice toward the subject and the audience
★ In informational text, look for main ideas and supporting details
★ Can summarize a story or chapter in text by retelling the key ideas and can sequence the events

★ Read to construct meaning, rather than to identify words, making fewer miscues as they read

Good readers know that great reading is more than just sounding out letters and words. They have developed systems to make meaning of text. Teachers can help students develop these systems with the strategies outlined in this book. Students become good readers when they learn to think about what they read to build their comprehension.

How to Instill a Can-Do Spirit: Teaching the Struggling Reader

Providing successful, scaffolded instruction for struggling readers is imperative in our classrooms today. However, teaching struggling readers can seem like an overwhelming and sometimes impossible task. Researchers estimate that with proper instruction, 95 percent of students can be taught to read properly (Duke & Pressley, 2005). It is so important to foster a can-do spirit in all readers and especially among struggling readers. Teachers must stress students' strengths and use their challenges as pathways to learning to overcome the obstacles to reading. Students must understand that they are *able*.

Let's think of the word *able* as an acronym. It helps educators design more inclusive lessons for all learners.

★ **Assessment:** The process begins with careful assessment. It is difficult to teach without knowing the student's entry point to learning. Assessment informs instruction.

★ **Building literacy skills:** Teachers need to build the students' literacy skills after the students are assessed. Many tools for building these skills are throughout this book.

★ **Linking strategies for transfer of learning:** Teachers also need to help struggling readers link reading strategies for transfer of learning. This occurs with frequent modeling and demonstrating of techniques so that strategies become routine for students. The focus needs to be on strategies that good readers use. This book has many examples of these techniques.

★ **Engagement:** Engagement is the key for reluctant readers. Using brain-based techniques is essential. Lecture and sit-and-get techniques are not motivating for struggling students. This book provides many ideas to interest students in the literacy process.

Final Thoughts

This book is about creating a blueprint for success for all students, including your struggling readers. The goal of this text is to provide a plethora of possibilities for teachers to build their own literacy program designed to look beyond the labels of struggling readers to what is more possible. If we look at our students with a new lens—that they are developing readers—there is hope. Their paths to becoming better readers will have challenges. This book provides you with tools for success that are adaptable and flexible enough to utilize with students of multiple ages and ability levels to meet those challenges.

2

Key Elements of Balanced Literacy Programs

If you were asked to create an effective program for all readers, and in particular, struggling readers, what elements would you include? This chapter helps teachers put the pieces of the puzzle together and structure a balanced literacy program. How do the components fit together to propel your students forward as better readers and writers? How do you weave effective instruction into each component to maximize the success of your students? In a truly balanced literacy program, it is about not just *what* you teach but also *how* you teach. Make each minute count in the instructional day because struggling readers don't have a minute to lose!

Research supports literacy instruction that addresses several aspects of the reading process in balance: phonics and the alphabetic code, fluency, comprehension, and vocabulary development. In their landmark report, *Preventing Reading Difficulties in Young Children* (Snow, Burns, & Griffin, 1998), the National Research Council notes that students need to understand the sound-symbol relationships of letters and words and must apply this understanding to read and spell words. In addition, they need to engage in wide reading and understand new vocabulary to boost fluency. Students also need to know what strategies to use so they can self-monitor as they read.

The National Reading Panel (2000) examines domains of effective literacy instruction and finds that reading programs should address phonemic awareness, phonics, fluency, vocabulary, and comprehension in the primary grades and have opportunities to connect reading and writing skills to text for older students (Ehri, 2003; Jitendra, Edwards, Sacks, & Jacobson, 2004; Rayner, Foorman, Perfetti, Pesetsky, & Seidenberg, 2001).

In developing an integrated literacy program, the following features need to be in place to support strategic instruction.

★ Teach critical skills and strategies to promote conceptual understanding.

★ Differentiate the content, process, and products required based on learners' specific needs using formative assessment techniques.

★ Provide explicit and systematic instruction and lots of time for repetition and practice in various contexts with ongoing support and feedback.

★ Scaffold instruction and provide opportunities for students to apply the skills and strategies in their independent reading by providing meaningful support.

★ Move beyond a curriculum of coverage to a curriculum of mastery by monitoring student progress regularly and reinforcing and reteaching when needed.

However, balance is not enough. It is necessary to purposefully and strategically integrate these components into a program of literacy instruction to prevent fragmentation of discrete skills and to provide opportunities for students to read and write meaningful and connected text. Effective teachers can adapt instruction to meet the diverse needs of their students, including struggling students, English learners, and advanced learners. Let's take a closer look at the essential components of effective programs for struggling readers.

Phonics Instruction

Research on struggling readers suggests that phonics is the most frequently cited skill that students lack (Kelly & Campbell, 2008). This knowledge of sound-symbol relationships is critical for reading success in the primary grades and beyond. Recognizing words in print and reading them with fluency depend on the foundation of phonics knowledge. A word needs to be deciphered first before students can attach meaning to it.

Focus on Fluency

Another important component of a literacy program is fluency. Students need to apply their phonics skills to acquire adequate fluency and automatic reading to comprehend the meaning of text. Struggling readers often read too slowly and labor over decoding, therefore compromising the meaning-making process. Fostering an independent reading level where a student recognizes more than 95 percent of the words is important.

Vocabulary Instruction

Teachers need to provide systematic and explicit instruction in the basic building blocks of the English language. Word study is an essential ingredient to a comprehensive literacy program. Knowledge of words is imperative for comprehension. During their elementary years, students are expected to learn several thousand word meanings per year (Learning First Alliance, 2000). Since most of these words are acquired by reading books or hearing them read aloud, wide reading and active processing of word meanings are important. Struggling readers need a broad exposure to a voluminous vocabulary.

Focus on Listening Comprehension

Listening is the most common communicative activity that we use in daily life; "we can expect to listen twice as much as we speak, four times more than we read, and five times more than we write" (Morley, 1991, p. 82). Therefore, it is vital that teachers emphasize listening comprehension in every literacy program. Listening comprehension is the receptive skill in the oral mode. When we speak of listening, what we really mean is listening and understanding what we hear. Teachers can enhance listening comprehension by using read-aloud and think-aloud strategies. In this way, teachers model how to figure out unknown words, the connection to text, and what comprehension looks like. Engaging students in an active discussion helps increase listening skills.

Focus on Text Comprehension

The purpose of learning to read is to comprehend content. Therefore, text comprehension is critical to the meaning-making process. Comprehension depends on having a working vocabulary and sufficient background knowledge to make connections to the content. Teachers can foster comprehension by modeling and through examining probing questions and encouraging students to question and discuss content with learning partners. This also helps students relate their own knowledge and experiences to the ideas in the text.

Focus on Written Expression

Another essential ingredient to an effective literacy program is written expression. A variety of opportunities for written expression develop effective communication skills. The building blocks to support struggling students in writing include letter formation, spelling, and sentence development. To support writers, teachers have students begin in the stages of generating and organizing their ideas with a learning partner, generating a draft, sharing ideas with others for peer feedback, and then moving on to revising, editing, and publishing their work.

Continuous Assessment

In order to monitor the progress of all students, a teacher must continuously assess learners to inform their instruction. Frequent, formative, and ongoing assessment of developing readers can prevent students from falling behind. Longitudinal studies indicate that students who are poor readers in third grade and beyond were having difficulty from the start with phonological skill development (Learning First Alliance, 2000). Interventions at an early age can prevent later reading failure and facilitate the literacy acquisition of most students.

School-Home Connection

School-home connections can enhance students' success in literacy development. Research supports the importance of reading at home (Carson, 1999; Gaskins, Ehri, Cress, O'Hara, & Donnelly, 1996; Learning First Alliance, 1998; Snow et al., 1998; Torgeson, 1998). In fact, when parents take the time to read to their children and help them read, they emphasize the importance of the reading process. Because of reading at home, children learn to love the sounds of language before they even notice the printed words on a page. Furthermore, reading books aloud to children stimulates their imagination and expands their understanding of the world. It helps them develop language and listening skills and prepares them to understand the written word.

The school-home connection is an excellent launchpad to literacy and developing strategic readers. Teachers must include these skills, strategies, and concepts as a necessary part of an effective literacy program. It is a matter of putting the pieces of the literacy puzzle together in the classroom. How do you identify and address the specific needs of your learners? Teachers need to explicitly teach strategies that students can use when they encounter difficulty. The following section provides building blocks to enhance literacy skills and develop strategic readers.

Developing Strategic Readers

Struggling readers respond well to direct and explicit instruction. Use the following guidelines to design instruction that involves the key elements described in the previous sections. Providing a broad range of literacy experiences gives students a pathway to comprehension.

Phonology and Word-Attack Skills: Guidelines for Phonological Awareness Instruction

Phonics involves the relationship between sounds and written symbols, and *phonemic awareness* involves the sounds in spoken words. Therefore, phonics instruction focuses on teaching sound-spelling relationships and is associated with print. Most phonemic awareness tasks are oral. This section looks at the principles of early-stage phonology teaching for students with moderate reading disabilities.

Increase Consistency and Redundancy

It is important to increase the consistency and redundancy of your lesson content, depending on the individual student's level of reading impairment. Use the same set of words in your lesson for decoding in phrases, sentences, and a passage.

If the student is reading at a low level, teach phonological awareness until the student can remember, state, and blend discrete speech sounds into a word. Students should also be able to segment speech sounds in a word using manipulatives.

Eliminate Letter Confusion

Another important technique for struggling readers is to eliminate letter confusion (*b, d, p, z* . . .). Address one confusing letter at a time. For example, teach *b* until the student can respond accurately to the letter-sound correspondence on a card, in a word, in text, and from dictation. Then teach *d* with the same intensity. Then combine the letters into small words on a piece of paper (for example, *bid, rib*). The strategy of screen spelling is described later in the book (see page 42) and will assist with reversals and help students experience letter development in a tactile way.

Monitor Text Difficulty

Consider monitoring the text level or text difficulty. If a student's accuracy decreases in a passage of text, first think about exactly what might be too difficult. Is a challenging element of the text impeding his or her progress? For example, if a student is reading at 89 percent accuracy, she is practicing decoding, not fluency, and the passage is not appropriate for fluency practice. The student should be reading at 95 percent or higher accuracy to practice fluency.

Assess at Regular Intervals

It is important to assess students at regular and frequent intervals. For example, manipulatives for segmentation are helpful in the assessment process. Give students counters, coins, or disks that are all of the same color or type. Students put a counter into a box for each phoneme or sound segment. Model the process by slowly stretching the word phoneme by phoneme. Gradually have the student "say it and move it" by taking turns placing counters in each box while saying each sound in a word (Elkonin, 1971). If students are experiencing difficulty, reduce the complexity of the language by limiting the number of syllables or phonemes. Use words that are already familiar to the students as part of their oral language.

Introduce Beginning Reading Skills Sooner

Do not wait until students have mastered phonemic awareness to introduce letter-sound relationships, sight vocabulary, and other beginning reading skills. Initial phoneme recognition and some segmentation ability are all students need to begin phonics instruction. For example, being able to isolate the first sound in a word should be sufficient for instruction in initial consonant correspondences (Lyon, 1999).

Phonological Memory Development: Listening and Looking Games

As Joanna Kellogg Uhry (2005) notes, students with dyslexia, a word-level reading disorder, typically memorize individual words but have difficulty generalizing from one word to another because of deficits in phonological awareness.

Verbal, short-term memory is a type of phonological process, as storage involves using phonological features. Young readers with difficulty in this type of phonological processing can decode letters to sounds but have difficulty remembering the sounds long enough to blend them into words. Therefore, it is not learning the letter-sound links that usually causes problems, but the ability to manipulate those discrete, identified sounds into meaningful words that is a challenge. To develop phonological memory in students, take the following steps.

Step One: Phonological Awareness

★ Ask students to listen for sound clues within words or nonsense words. Hold up one finger for each syllable in the word (or clap your hands once for each syllable).

★ Say the word, syllable by syllable, and ask students to "put down a counter" (such as a colored disk) for each "tiny sound," or phoneme, they hear (sounds, not letters).

★ For older students, use vocabulary from content-area learning, such as words from a science unit.

Step Two: Orthographic Awareness

★ Using the same words as in step one, have students identify the spelling units (one- or two- letter clusters) in the words from memory if they are able.

★ Present the word on a card and ask students to look carefully at each letter. Allow one second per letter.

★ Cover the card or turn it over. Ask students to close their eyes and form a picture of the word in their mind's eye. If working with a small group, have students tell you the spelling units. If the group is large, students may write them down.

★ Ask the students to identify the spelling unit in specific positions in the word and sometimes the whole word—for example, the first and third letter, the third and fourth, the third and fifth, and so on.

★ In later sessions, you may provide a word list for each student. Ask them to run their fingers under the word, focusing in on each letter; cover the word with a card; and then spell it aloud.

Step Three: Decoding

★ Ask students to segment, blend, and identify each spelling unit and rewrite in alternate colors (red and blue, for example) if they have trouble. Follow with instruction in larger units.

★ Phoneme segmentation is one of the later-developing skills in students. Have students begin by segmenting single syllables with two or three sounds without blends (such as *cat*: /c/a/t/) and gradually have them segment three- to four-phoneme words including blends (such as *black*: /b/l/a/k/). After you assess your students and identify those who need extra help with this skill, reinforce the skill with manipulatives.

★ Use the break-up words activity to reinforce decoding. Have each student identify one-to-one correspondence, matching the number of dots on a card with the number of sounds in a word. Be sure to provide a lot of modeling and practice during this part of your intervention program. You can gradually decrease the amount of prompting you provide as the students improve.

Support Strategies for Struggling Readers: Pause-Prompt-Praise

Once your struggling readers have improved their phonemic awareness and sound segmentation abilities, introduce additional techniques and strategies to enhance and enrich their literacy skills. The main purpose of reading is to glean meaning from text. Strategic readers effectively monitor their comprehension as they read and are able to self-correct if what they read does not make sense, sound right, or look right in the book.

One strategy to try is the pause-prompt-praise strategy when students come to an unfamiliar word and start to struggle. This process encourages students to self-correct and monitor the meaning of the text as they read.

Step One: Pause

If the student makes a mistake while reading, first pause. Then wait, giving the student "think time" and a chance to solve the problem.

Step Two: Prompt

General Prompts

Direct student attention to possible sources of information in the text. Ask, "What can you do to figure out the word?" You could prompt the student with, "Something puzzled you. Start here [point with a pencil to a place in text, the beginning of a phrase, or a sentence]." Continue with any of the following prompts.

★ Ask the student to sound the first letter, the first sound, and then the whole word out loud.

★ Ask the student to break the word into parts (syllables).

★ Point to a picture related to the word.

★ Ask questions about the book related to the word.

★ Provide a similar word or a rhyming word as a hint.

★ Read the whole sentence through to the end, leaving the unknown words as a gap. Ask the student to fill in the gap.

Specific Prompts

Give the student directions. Focus on a word identification strategy and provide context support. For example, prompt the student by saying, "Touch and say each sound. Cover up part of the word so you can see the chunk. Find a part you know." Additional support could include the following.

★ If the student stops at an unknown word and cannot continue, ask him or her to read on to the end of the sentence and try again.

★ If the student makes a substitution that does not make sense, prompt him or her by asking a question about the meaning of the story using context clues.

★ If the student makes a substitution that does not look right, prompt with a question about the way the word looks, and ask about which part of the word might look wrong or doesn't fit.

★ If the word is not correct after two prompts, say the word. For reinforcement, write the word on a whiteboard, use magnetic letters, or use the screen spelling technique (described in chapter 3).

Step Three: Praise and Reinforce

To reinforce the successful strategy from steps one and two and encourage future application, restate how the student used the strategy. Have the student verbalize what he or she did as well. For example, you could say, "You went back and tried it again. You broke the word into chunks. The way you used a part of the word that you knew already to help you say the whole word was great. Tell me how you did that. Let's try it again." Be specific in your praise so that the student knows what he or she did correctly.

★ "Great! You did that by yourself."

★ "Good job sounding out the letters."

★ "Wow, you solved that problem!"

★ "You get a 'Well done!' for trying new words."

Using Higher-Level Thinking Skills

Think of your typical instructional day. What kind of tasks do you ask students to perform? Richard Allington (2012) finds that many teachers focus on low-level skills instead of the higher-level thinking skills that can engage reluctant readers. Very little learning transfers when a student spends the instructional day on low-level tasks like locating, matching, copying, and listing. These tasks do not develop the meaning-making process that is critical for comprehension.

Teachers need to utilize higher-level skills that result in greater transfer, such as paraphrasing, explaining, inferring, synthesizing, summarizing, and clarifying. The implications of this research are quite clear: teachers need to be more explicit in directly teaching reading strategies so that students can become more engaged and purposeful in the reading process. Teach students to describe the purpose of the reading by asking, "Why do you need to read _____?" Setting a purpose for reading is the process of identifying and stating clearly *why* you want to read. Teachers can model higher-level thinking skills by modeling think-aloud strategies such as setting a purpose before students try the same strategies with a learning partner.

Making Sense of Text

To make sense of text, good readers determine the importance of what they are reading, summarize information, make inferences, generate questions, and monitor their comprehension. Teachers can use the following methods to help students make meaning of what they read throughout the three stages of the reading process. Make sure students understand what the purpose for reading is to get the main idea, obtain specific information, understand the content, or enjoy a story. Recognizing the purpose for reading will help students select appropriate reading strategies.

Before Reading

This is a critical phase in the reading process. As you set the stage for reading, you should create a need to know on the part of the learner. Prereading activities help struggling students tap into their prior knowledge, interact with portions of the text, practice strategies such as sequencing and predicting, and identify challenging vocabulary words. Ask students to think about what they already know about the topic. They can share their ideas verbally or in pictures. Show the cover of the text and ask students to predict what the text will be about. Record their responses.

While Reading

Ask questions continuously throughout teacher read-aloud, or have students pause, reflect, and make connections during their independent or paired reading with learning partners.

You can preselect several stopping points within the text for students to ask and answer questions. This is also an opportunity to model "fix-it strategies" to correct any confusions students might have. Some questions to pose during the reading process include:

★ What do I understand from what I just read?
★ What is the main idea?
★ What picture is the author painting?
★ Do I need to reread so that I understand?

Encourage students to ask their own questions after you have modeled this strategy, and record their questions on chart paper. You can group students to answer one another's questions and generate new ones based on their discussions. Be sure that the focus is on making connections to the text and asking thoughtful questions. Students should ask and answer questions that:

★ Will lead to a deeper understanding of the text
★ Have answers that can be found in the text
★ Clarify meaning and the author's intent
★ Help them make predictions and inferences
★ Help them make connections to other texts or prior knowledge

As students begin to read more independently, continue to model the questioning process and encourage students to use it often as they read independently or with learning partners. Ask students to look for answers to the questions they have as they read. Have them predict what will happen next in the story and relate what they are reading to their background and prior knowledge. Instruct students to check for meaning by rereading parts that aren't making sense. Prompt students to use context clues to determine a new word or the meaning of a word. Invite students to retell parts of the story. For visual learners, ask students to describe the pictures the story inspires in their mind. Promote the use of graphic organizers to make sense of text (see chapter 5). Have the students draw conclusions and inferences based on what they have read.

After Reading

This is the time for your students to recall and reflect on what they read and summarize the key points. Ask students to retell the important points in the text. Ask students to dramatize a chunk of text for the class. Or ask students to transform the story, taking the characters into another time, changing characters completely, creating a different ending, adapting the story to a different genre, and so on. Visual learners could create a storyboard to graph and chart the main points of the story.

Thinking Aloud

To get students to "think about their thinking," many teachers model the think-aloud strategy as a classroom comprehension technique (Davey, 1983; Nist & Kirby, 1986). A *think-aloud* is a strategy in which the teacher reads aloud from a text and verbalizes his or her thoughts, questions, comments, predictions, and reactions to show students what readers do in their minds during the actual reading phase. This promotes reading as an active process of engagement. Take the following steps to implement this technique.

★ **Select a passage for modeling:** Select a short passage of one hundred to three hundred words to read aloud to students.

★ **Prepare your comments to share:** Keep in mind that your purpose is to model your connections to the text as you pause when you read and pose questions to the students.

★ **Explain the technique to students:** Tell the students that you are going to share what you think about as you read. (Students should have a copy of the text in front of them.)

★ **Read the passage and use think-aloud strategies:** Share the passage that you selected, and stop whenever you have a connection, question, or response. According to Beth Davey (1983), you can include—

   ✦ Making predictions
   ✦ Visualizing
   ✦ Sharing connections with prior knowledge
   ✦ Demonstrating how to verbalize a confusing point
   ✦ Modeling strategies, such as self-correcting or rereading for emphasis or to focus on meanings of the words

   Have students keep a list of the different types of things you (the reader) are doing as you read to help you better understand the text.

★ **Discuss the think-aloud strategy and answer student questions:** When you're done, start a master list on a large piece of paper, writing down strategies that the students observed you doing during the think-aloud, using their own words.

★ **Provide practice with learning partners:** Have students select a passage to read from their text or story. They should read the passage individually first, keeping in mind the strategies you modeled for them. They should pause, reflect, and think about what they read, referring to the master strategy list and discussing the strategies they used. Add to the list if possible. Then encourage students to verbalize their thoughts as they read aloud, taking turns with their learning partner.

Why is the think-aloud process so important? Suzanne Wade (1990) investigated the impact of the think-aloud strategy as a process to assess students' reading comprehension. She concludes that there are four types of text comprehenders: (1) good comprehenders, (2) nonrisk takers, (3) schema imposers, and (4) storytellers. Wade finds that students may not always share what they are aware of in their reading or be able to verbalize it because they have had limited practice in describing their thinking processes, making the think-aloud strategy critical to model and practice with your students.

How do you get your students ready to think? Ready to make predictions? The think-before-you-read activity sheet (figure 2.1) assists students in becoming more actively engaged in making predictions and thinking more deeply about the text they are going to read. You can use this strategy first before starting the think-aloud process.

Think-Before-You-Read Activity Sheet

In textbooks, look at pictures and illustrations, maps and charts, captions, chapter titles, section titles, and bold words, and then focus on the first things and last things the chapter says.

In storybooks, describe the picture on the cover, read the text on the back cover, look over chapter titles and the beginning page of the book, and read any prologue or introduction.

Next, finish each sentence and then add one or two more sentences of your own.

• After I look at the reading, I predict that I will be reading about . . .
_____

• I already know something about this topic. I know that . . .
_____
_____
_____
_____
_____

• Something I don't know about this topic and would like to find out more about is . . .
_____
_____
_____
_____

Figure 2.1: Activity to assist students in becoming more actively involved in thinking deeply about text.

- What I can do when I can't read the textbook is . . .

_____

_____

_____

_____

_____

- -

Support Strategies for Teachers

1. Provide supplemental resources on the topic at a more accessible reading level.

2. Modify the text by:

   ☐ Using graphic organizers to focus reading (see chapter 5)

   ☐ Highlighting key portions of the text

   ☐ Making comments in the margin using sticky notes

   ☐ Building background knowledge through images, video clips, preteaching, and so on

   ☐ Listening to taped portions of the text or modified versions of the text (played on an MP3 player or iPod)

   ☐ Modeling and demonstrating the major themes

   ☐ Reading it using guided reading groups, shared reading, interactive groups, choral reading or echo, and so on

   ☐ Reading to learning partners using jigsaw, reciprocal reading, read-around groups (students taking turns reading), and so on

   ☐ Reviewing content frequently to assist in the sequence for students having difficulty following the storyline

   ☐ Providing copies of reading material with main ideas underlined or high-lighted

   ☐ Introducing new words by connecting how the words are related to the meaning of the text

   ☐ Using an index card or paper strip to keep your place on the page and to facilitate tracking

*Visit **go.SolutionTree.com/literacy** for a free reproducible version of this figure.*

Final Thoughts

Always think about the continuum of diverse learners in your classroom and what strategies will help students maximize their success in reading. Reaching all learners requires extra effort; however, the strategies in this chapter take little prep time and are effective in general education or special education classrooms. They are designed to be successful with all ages and ability levels K–8. Differentiation is not a magic wand, though; it is all about dedicating yourself to meeting the individual needs of all students who walk through your classroom door.

Let's move forward with more ideas about how to make this happen. The next chapter focuses on early literacy intervention.

3 Effective Early Literacy Intervention

Strong fundamental literacy skills are essential for student success and ongoing reading proficiency. Effective early literacy instruction involves many considerations, including developmentally appropriate settings and classrooms, a print-rich environment with adequate materials and resources, and a supportive learning environment where literacy can flourish. To help them become better readers, young students need to be read to, they need writing to help them learn about reading, they need reading to help them learn about writing, and they need oral language to help them learn about both reading and writing (Roskos, Christie, & Richgels, 2003). Furthermore, in the early literacy stages, it is important to integrate play to make literacy activities more meaningful and engaging for students. Effective early literacy intervention integrates these elements into the broader communication network that students need to make sense of their experiences, their world, and the texts that they encounter.

Early Intervention Strategies

What should students know and be able to do to help them succeed in literacy development in the primary grades? Learning to read and write is of critical importance in academic achievement and success in life. To ensure that every student becomes a competent reader and writer is a responsibility shared by teachers and students' families.

The role that teachers play in early literacy instruction is to teach basic skills and to provide meaningful, creative, and engaging classroom experiences supported by inclusive teaching practices. Each student comes to the classroom with a different background and different abilities. Teachers need to consider students' individual needs and provide balanced programs with explicit instruction and meaningful reading and writing tasks (Slegers, 1996).

Make Time to Talk

Involving students in robust conversations in a whole group, in a small group, and with learning partners is important. Pay attention to the words you use with young students. Try using unique and rare words to extend their listening vocabulary beyond the conversational words they are used to hearing. Students should also be encouraged to extend their own comments into more descriptive and detailed statements. Discuss challenging content in ways that involve knowledge of the larger world. Above all, listen and respond to what students have to say.

Read, Read, Read . . .

It is essential to read aloud to your students at least twice a day. This practice exposes them not only to numerous entertaining and informative stories, poems, and informational text but also to the rhythm and cadence of language. Take time for supportive conversations before, during, and after you read aloud to give students time to reflect and make connections to the text. Repeated reading (of favorite texts) impacts struggling readers in a positive way by improving fluency (Kita, 2011), which leads to comprehension.

Promote Phonics Fun

Think of multiple ways to expose your students to the sounds of language. Phonological awareness is at the foundation of learning to read, so play sound games, listen to stories together, and share poems and songs. Provide activities that increase students' awareness of the sounds of language that involve:

★ **Rhyme**—For example, use picture cards that represent rhyming words so students say the word and then match it with the rhyming word.
★ **Alliteration**—For example, teach tongue twisters, pointing out how to recognize when several words begin with the same sound.
★ **Sound matching**—For example, show students pictures and ask which picture begins with a certain letter sound.

Be sure to make these activities fun and engaging.

Unpack the ABCs

Engage students with multimodal materials that promote letter and word identification, including:

★ ABC books
★ Magnetic letters
★ Alphabet blocks
★ Puzzles
★ Alphabet charts

Teach letter names explicitly and make personal connections so that the process is more meaningful. For example, "Look, Tony and Tina's names both start with the same letter! What letter is that? What sound does that letter make?"

Provide an Environment Rich in Literacy

Provide a literacy-rich environment that encourages students to try to read books and other printed materials, including:

★ An abundant library center stocked with a variety of books from different genres

★ Several copies of favorite books for repeated readings to encourage independent reading

★ Examples of functional print materials linked to class activities (such as daily schedules, morning messages, helper charts, learning center schedules, and so on)

★ A variety of print resources from the real world (for example, menus, signs, magazines, and so on)

Support Emergent Writing

Students need to be encouraged to express themselves in writing at an early age, including through scribble writing, random letter formations, phonetic spelling to tell stories, and so on. Ways to promote early writing development in your students include:

★ Establishing a writing center, stocked with writing resources, pens, paper, crayons, and book-making supplies

★ Modeling shared writing demonstrations by eliciting responses from students and then writing them down on a chart, on a whiteboard, or on sentence strips for all to see

★ Providing functional writing opportunities related to the classroom community and activities throughout the day, including sign-up sheets for learning centers, morning messages, library book check-out cards, various classroom signs, and so on

★ Incorporating writing into play activities as part of learning centers or dramatic play—for example, writing directions to their favorite playground, taking orders for a restaurant play center, writing a pretend script for a radio commercial, and so on

Use Interactive, Shared Reading

Reading big books or other enlarged texts to a small group or as a whole-class activity is a very engaging literacy activity if students interact as the teacher models reading. Point to the print as you read it aloud. Encourage students to read along, particularly when the book is a favorite and is read repeatedly in class, so students gain confidence. Ask some students to act out a few of their favorite parts of the story.

As you read, point out concepts of print.

★ Left-to-right progression
★ Top-to-bottom orientation
★ What to look for in pictures versus print (What do pictures tell about the story?)
★ Features of the text, such as the cover, title, and so on

A Look at the World Through Literacy

In your balanced literacy program for emergent readers, make sure that you include integrated, content-focused activities. It is important to provide opportunities for your students to dig deeper into special topics that interest them. The purpose is for students to use many literacy skills, such as oral language, reading, and writing, in their examination of the world around them. Such investigation enriches students' language and literacy skills, and they gather valuable real-world background knowledge.

Some favorite topics for young students to explore might include cats and dogs, brothers and sisters, birthdays, ice cream, scary stuff, dancing, bicycles, holidays, the beach, dinosaurs, bugs, and so on. Once students have identified their topics, provide multiple literacy opportunities to explore, such as:

★ Listening to books and articles on the topic being read aloud
★ Reading books on their own
★ Gathering additional information and data from photographs, observations, interviews, and so on
★ Developing their emergent writing skills as they reflect on the pictures, text, observations, and so on
★ Engaging in dramatic play to express what they're learning in creative ways

Word Decoding

Teach word decoding strategies during independent or guided reading or during shared reading time. Send a copy of the strategies home to parents so they can reinforce these techniques at home as well to reinforce the school-home connection.

★ **Look at the picture:** Sometimes an unfamiliar word can be determined by looking at a picture in the book.
★ **Look for chunks in the word:** These are small parts of the word that the student might recognize, such as /at/ in *cat* and /ing/ in *bring*.
★ **Get your mouth ready:** The student should form the first letter of the word and then make the sound of the letter as he or she gets ready to read the word.

- ★ **Read, skip, read:** If the student is stuck on a word, he or she should *skip* the word and *read on* to the end of the sentence. By reading the other words in context, the student can often figure out the unknown word.
- ★ **Cross-check:** If the student does say a wrong word while reading aloud, the student should practice cross-checking. Students should ask themselves—
    - ✦ Does it look right?
    - ✦ Does it sound right?
    - ✦ Does it make sense?

A Focus on Strengths

As a former special education teacher and literacy coach, I am always eager to emphasize the importance of focusing on strengths—not just student weaknesses. Here are some things to consider.

- ★ **Notice students' strengths:** Often teachers and parents are consumed by a student's deficits and don't take time to notice his or her strengths. If a student is artistic, have her draw the main idea of the story. If he is verbal, have him retell the story in his own words. Letting a student use his or her talents will boost confidence and reinforce what the student is doing well.
- ★ **Celebrate every success:** It is important to affirm even the smallest accomplishments because you don't want to rely on report card grades as the only judge of a student's achievement. Maybe a student can read one word correctly that she did not know the day before. Maybe the student can self-correct an error—praise him! Struggling readers (and all readers) need to be reminded about what they are doing right, not just made aware of their mistakes.
- ★ **Set realistic goals:** For success with literacy, take it one step at a time. Set achievable and believable short-term, concrete goals. It is helpful to use the SMART Goals Framework (Doran, 1981) when developing specific goals for your students. Goals should be specific; measurable; attainable; relevant, rigorous, realistic, and results-focused; and timely and trackable.
- ★ **Don't let poor spelling impact progress:** Even poor spellers have important ideas to express. Students can use adaptive devices, such as text-prediction software or spell-checkers. Getting thoughts down on paper is more important for beginning readers than accuracy in spelling during the early grades.
- ★ **Share your own challenges:** Share some things that you are not terrific at doing. Admitting that you also struggle with something is a way of providing support. For example, I am spatially challenged and have difficulty

telling right from left when giving directions. It's important for students to know that everyone has weaknesses.

* **Read aloud daily:** Emphasize to students and their families that struggling readers should be read to every day. They need to hear the language to develop oral fluency, and it sparks their creativity and interest. You can boost their listening comprehension without the struggles of decoding the text. In addition, they build background knowledge and can visualize and use their imagination. While reading, occasionally pause and question to allow the student to make connections and predictions.

* **Small steps can make a big difference:** Keep the process simple. When students are beginning readers, encourage students and parents to review the alphabet and beginning sounds. Break apart short CVC words and have students slowly blend those sounds together (/c/a/t/ = *cat*).

* **Teach students how to help themselves:** Give students tools they can use when they are stuck. Teach them how to ask for help and how to understand their strengths and weaknesses so that they can advocate for themselves. They will feel more confident in school, and they will know what they need to do to keep up.

Instructional Interventions for Young Struggling Readers

The most important way to improve literacy instruction for struggling readers and students at risk of reading failure is to start early. This section provides carefully constructed scaffolding strategies for emerging readers and writers. These interventions are all classroom tested, are easy to implement, and have proven effective with the diverse learners and struggling students with whom I have worked during my career as an educator.

* As a foundational reading skill, students need to be able to match the written word with the spoken word. This is called *one-to-one matching*.
  + Use two fingers to frame the word (one finger at the beginning of the word and the other finger at the end of the word). This helps the student focus in on the isolated word to sound it out.
  + Say, "Read it with your finger" or "Did that match?" Pointing is a strategy that promotes one-to-one correspondence—the ability to match written word to spoken word while reading. The student or teacher slides a finger underneath the word while reading.

* Have the student generate sentences, cut them up, and reconstruct them. This sequencing of words to create meaningful thoughts helps enhance students' phrasing and fluency. Ask the student to compose a one- to two-sentence story. First, write the words on a long sentence strip as the

student says them. For example, a student might suggest the sentence, "I like to walk my dog in the park." Then cut up the sentence word by word while the student watches. Next, the student reassembles the sentence and reads it. Place the word pieces in an envelope with the sentence written on the outside. The student can then reassemble the sentence at a later time.

★ Point along with the student as he or she reads, and pause when he or she makes a mistake that can be corrected.

★ Clap out written or oral sentences and count the number of words. First, model how to clap the word chunks (syllables) and then the whole words. Then students clap independently.

★ Hold the student's hand to guide his or her pointing, or use a variety of pointers—for example, chopsticks, wands, or rubber fingertips. The teacher models how to use the pointer, and then the student uses the pointer independently.

★ Select books with very few words on a page to begin the reading lessons with struggling students.

★ Highlight each word with a different color. First, demonstrate how to highlight the words, and then have the student follow.

Build Decoding and Word-Attack Skills

If a student has trouble decoding or lacks word-attack skills:

★ Do a variety of word sorts using word chips. A word sort is a developmental word study activity that is referenced in the *Words Their Way* curriculum (Bear, 2000). The activity is a hands-on approach to focusing the student on critical features of words, namely sound, pattern, and meaning. Word sorts can be quite simple, very complex, and anywhere in between. For beginning and struggling readers, having words to manipulate and sort helps reinforce the concepts being taught. For example, students might sort word families to help them recognize word patterns and learn about onset and rime. First, ask students to select a vowel, and then present them with a series of words to sort into short-vowel word families. Students can then print their completed word family chart and use it to practice reading the words fluently.

★ Use assorted word-attack skill games with a learning partner or instructional assistant. For example, play sight-word bingo with frequently used words. Another strategy is to bring your word wall to life with a flyswatter. Call out a question related to one of the words on the wall, and then have a student find it, swat it, and say it.

★ Allow many opportunities to read and reread books that are easy for the student in a variety of genres so he or she can practice and experience success in building word mastery and increasing fluency.

★ Use picture books that use a repetitive phonological pattern.

★ Give the student ample time to analyze a word instead of giving the answer immediately.

★ Teach the student to look for and underline known words.

★ Model and use prompts that lead to independent strategies; ask the student, "Are there any chunks you know? Can you get your mouth ready? What else can you do?"

Build Vocabulary Skills

If a student has a limited vocabulary:

★ Encourage the student to brainstorm with other students for synonyms and antonyms.

★ Have the student keep a word book of new words he or she has learned.

★ Play games that build word knowledge, like Password. To prepare for the game, determine a set of vocabulary words at the students' reading level. These words become the passwords students find during game play. Give students game cards containing one-word clues to describe each password to their partners. Students give each other the one-word clues as their partners try to guess the passwords.

★ Provide many objects from everyday life to talk about, and develop new words to describe them. For instance, a ball could be described as round, squishy, soft, and so on.

★ Use picture cards for sorting and categorizing. There are multiple ways to sort picture cards, including:
   + Rhyming words
   + Words that start with the same sound
   + People, places, and things
   + Long-vowel words and short-vowel words
   + Alphabetized words
   + Opposites

★ Use picture books with no words and encourage students to tell the story, adding their own words.

★ Provide a print-rich and visually rich environment with "walls of wonder" so there is no escape from learning. Display word walls of frequently used words around the room. Design interactive walls on which students must locate rhyming words, words that have certain sounds, words that contain blends, and so on. You might, for example, mount empty cereal boxes and other interesting print materials on the wall for students to search for these elements. Create opportunities for students to interact with many forms of print, including signs, stories, word displays, murals, bulletin boards, charts, poems, and student work samples.

Build Sound-Symbol Relationship Skills

If a student has problems remembering sound-symbol relationships:

★ Start with the familiar—sounds in the student's name and then names of family and friends.

★ Display a name chart of all the students' names. Use other names to gradually increase the level of difficulty. You can do word-wall activities where students locate names that rhyme, names that have blends, names with digraphs, and so on.

★ Read simple, decodable text at first to increase student confidence and success.

★ Use manipulatives to reinforce sound-symbol relationships, such as letter cards, magnetic letters, *Scrabble* tiles, pocket charts, and so on.

★ Develop anchor cue cards with pictures for each letter-sound spelling so that students can associate an image with a sound.

★ Ask the students to vocalize the sounds as they write.

★ Make an ABC book with only the letters the student recognizes; gradually add to the book as he or she learns new sounds. Send the book home so that parents can reinforce sound-symbol relationships.

★ 9Use raps, rhythms, and rhymes to reinforce letter sounds. Teachers model these using vocabulary, and then students can work in small groups to develop their own.

★ Teach phonics-related skills in the context of relevant words, phrases, and sentences so the words become more meaningful to students.

★ Have the students work in pairs to create a letter collage. For example, if a pair has the letter B, they find pictures from magazines of things that start with B, cut them out, and glue them onto their poster paper to create a collage.

★ Stretch out the word using a large rubber band as a prop. Get a thick, sturdy rubber band. Stretch the rubber band between your fingers. Sound out a word, and as you do so, stretch the band out so that the student can visually see how sounds stretch out into words.

Build Sight/Word Skills

If the student has difficulty with sight words:

★ Highlight high-frequency words. Students can dictate a short story or a response to a question. Write the sentences they speak on a sentence strip, and highlight the sight word you want to emphasize.

★ Give students repeated opportunities to practice fluency.

* Encourage students to say, write, and read words many times to develop automaticity.
* Develop word banks of sight words for students to create sentences.
* Use analogy comparisons to help students see similarities and differences among printed words.
* Make sure that unfamiliar words are used in context so students can try to infer meaning.
* Have students create flash cards of unfamiliar words for reinforcement and practice.
* Build and break apart words with magnetic letters.
* Have students create a picture dictionary.
* Have students work with learning partners to create word puzzles with the word on one piece of paper and the definition on another. Once the students have completed their puzzle pieces, mix them up and deal them out to students. Each student attempts to match his or her word or definition with its other piece. Model this activity before asking students to match the pieces.
* Label objects in the classroom using single target words or sentences.
* Play the game of Concentration with words and meanings.
* Play sight-word bingo.
* Focus on useful, meaningful sight words first, such as familiar names, days of the week, months, and so on.

Build Skills for Context Clues

If a student has a problem using context clues to identify words:

* Encourage students to insert words that make sense as they read if they can't read a particular word or don't know its meaning.
* Use the *cloze procedure*—a comprehension activity where words are omitted from a passage and students must fill in the blanks.
* Provide a wide variety of genres and assorted reading materials, including predictable books, trade books, magazines, newspapers, student writing, and so on.
* Teach students to read until the end of the sentence—to not cut it short; provide clues for students to look for in the text.
* Practice listening for miscues using teacher read-aloud with intentional and obvious errors; students indicate when the miscues occur and why they think there is an error.
* Teach students to recognize and use a variety of context clues to gain meaning from text, including association clues, synonym clues, experience clues, and comparison-or-contrast clues.

★ Make a deck of function word flash cards (*as*, *a*, *an*, *and*, *the*); use pictures to cue students to make phrases using the function words.

★ Use irrelevant words; create sentences with extra, unneeded words; and have students read the sentences and delete the extra words.

Build Self-Monitoring Skills

If a student does not self-monitor as he or she reads:

★ Model self-monitoring through a think-aloud process.

★ Talk about what to do when encountering an unknown word before starting to read independently.

★ Ask students to reinforce their reading with one-to-one pointing or tracking.

★ Develop a strategies chart so students can indicate what strategies they are using during reading.

★ Direct the student's attention to meaning.

★ After a student error, ask probing questions such as, "What was the hard part?"

★ Cover up a word that was misread; ask students, "What would you expect to see at the beginning of the word _____? Does this word start like that? Please try again."

★ When the student hesitates or pauses, ask the student, "Why did you stop?" or "What did you notice?" Be specific in your feedback to provide a teachable moment.

★ Praise and recognize efforts at self-monitoring: "I like the way you tried to make meaning there."

★ Actively respond to students while they are reading: "You read it this way. Does that make sense? Is that the way we talk? Try it again, please."

★ Modify or adjust the reading materials or text content to the student's reading level.

Build Comprehension Skills

If a student demonstrates poor comprehension skills:

★ Start by building the student's background knowledge, concept development, and oral language skills.

★ Activate the student's schema through a teacher think-aloud.

★ Develop automaticity and word recognition skills because comprehension breaks down with poor decoding skills, lack of fluency, and a slow reading rate.

★ Provide direct instruction in understanding story schema and story elements; read a variety of stories with standard structures to facilitate the student's ability to predict or anticipate.

★ Match books to students' reading level and interests; when reading materials are too difficult, student attention is focused on decoding and not on the meaning of the passage.

★ Make sure that the student is aware of how punctuation provides signals to aid comprehension; practice interpreting these marks.

★ Model metacognition and prediction checks during reading.

★ Teach cause-effect relationships.

★ After reading, do story-frame activities, including story summary, story maps, character analysis, and comparison.

★ Teach students to recognize sequence and time-order signal words that will help them glean meaning from text.

★ Practice locating details and main ideas in a newspaper story, answering who, what, where, why, and when questions.

★ Make a cloze story map by placing the main idea in the center of the map and connecting key words for major concepts or events.

★ Have the students sequence pictures from the story: beginning, middle, and end.

★ Utilize prereading strategies and activities: previews, anticipation guides, and concept mapping.

★ Teach students to make use of paragraphs that have specific functions; use summary paragraphs to check their memory.

★ Use reciprocal teaching to promote comprehension monitoring: predicting, question generating, summarizing, and clarifying.

Build Skills for Making Inferences and Drawing Conclusions

If a student has difficulty making inferences or drawing conclusions:

★ Model a think-aloud lesson.

★ Solve short mysteries together as part of a class discussion.

★ Look at a collection of pictures or objects and ask students to make connections among them and create stories using them.

★ Listen to a story and predict what will happen next.

★ Underline or highlight word or phrase clues that lead to making an inference.

Build Skills for Finding the Main Idea

If a student has difficulty finding the main idea:

★ Ask students to write a paragraph and give it a title that tells the main idea.

★ Ask students to categorize objects, pictures, words, and sentences; have them name the category and explain why the objects or pictures go together.

★ Have students observe you modeling ways to identify the main idea—what the selection is mostly about.

★ Ask students to choose an advertisement, using the product as the main idea, and select several features of the product as the details.

★ Read a paragraph in which one sentence does not belong, lead a class discussion about which sentence does not belong and why, and remove the sentence and describe the main idea and why that sentence does not belong.

★ Point out that the main idea or topic sentence usually contains *who*, *what*, *where*, *when*, or *how*.

★ Bring in articles from the newspaper and cut out several headlines, have students match the appropriate article with the matching title, and talk about what clues assisted them in the matching process.

Build Skills for Structural Analysis

If a student lacks awareness of structural analysis while reading:

★ Create a cloze passage to practice with that has missing morphemes.

★ Provide students with a variety of interesting reading materials, and model features to look for in structural analysis.

★ Underline the root words on a list with affixes.

★ Count the number of syllables in a spoken word by clapping, tapping a pencil, or holding up fingers for each sound pronounced.

★ Provide sample sentences with word choices; the students select the word with the correct suffix—for example, "The boy _____ (walk, walks, walked, walking) along the riverbank."

★ Create words using a flip chart that contains root words in the center, prefixes at the beginning, and suffixes at the end.

★ Ask students to sort picture cards into categories for one-syllable words, two-syllable words, and so on.

★ Use manipulative letters so that students can be aware of root words by making them and breaking them apart.

★ Use the word wall as a launchpad to learning by asking, "What's my rule?" drawing attention to the word's structure (a silent *e*, double consonants, vowel teams, and so on).

★ Cut up student-generated sentences at critical points to emphasize chunking; then have the students reassemble and reread the sentences ("Where would I cut off the word *friendly* to leave off the /ly/ chunk?").

★ Assess the student's awareness of structure (blends, digraphs, and so on), and use extended activities to teach, model, and practice.

★ Play prefix or suffix *Jeopardy!*

★ Play What's My Rule? using your classroom word wall; select two words and ask the students to tell you the rule for putting those two words together.

★ Play compound-word concentration, where students build compound words and match them with pictures in a pocket chart or put together compound-word puzzles.

★ Make sure you provide ample practice so that students recognize letters and produce sounds of phonemes with fluency and automaticity.

★ Teach students to use the circle, circle, underline strategy when decoding multisyllabic words (circle the prefix, circle the suffix, and underline the vowels in the root word); if this activity is done on a regular basis, it will increase students' ability to break down and understand multisyllabic words.

★ Distribute word cards to students to practice compound-word development, and have them look for their learning partners to create a compound word; the partners share their words with the rest of the class.

★ Play team word building. (Divide the class into two teams. Give each team an equal number of root word cards. For example, a student from team A displays a card and calls on a member of team B. That student needs to name at least three words that use that root word plus an affix. If not, that student joins team A. However, if the student can name those words, he or she selects a member from team A to join team B. This is played until all the cards are used or until all players are on one team.)

Build Fluency

If a student reads word by word or lacks fluency:

★ Reread easy books, songs, and poems so that students feel successful.

★ Use choral reading by pairing less-fluent readers with fluent students as they read selected passages in unison; this builds confidence for at-risk readers.

★ Use echo reading, where the student echoes your oral rendition, one sentence or phrase at a time. (Begin by recording the student reading the passage or phrase. Then record the echo read. Finally, record a third reading by individual struggling students. This process allows the student to compare results and note improvement.)

★ Make sure that the text is appropriate for a student's speaking and listening vocabulary.

★ Use text chunking to show phrase boundaries in a text or passage by making slash marks; then have students read it aloud.

★ Use reader's theater. (This technique gives students an opportunity to work as a group and to practice and demonstrate fluency. Each student or group of students is given a specific role to dramatize for the class. This is particularly effective for stories that students find familiar.)

★ Use repeated readings—one of the most effective ways of improving fluency; the passages should be of high interest to the students to increase engagement.

★ Read from different genres to create different moods and show a variety of voice (prosody).

★ Use familiar reading daily. (Give each student a book box or book basket of familiar texts that students can read independently. Repeated reading of text that they have used during guided reading sessions will increase their reading rates.)

★ Use the neurological impress method. (Read slightly ahead of the student. As the student gains mastery and increases fluency, your voice "shadows" just behind the student's. This technique also works well to increase the reading skills of English learners.)

Build Skills to Avoid Reversal

If a student makes reversals:

★ Have the student trace a word or letter from left to right, following the direction of an arrow at the top of the page or word card.

★ Print a word, making the first letter green (go) and the last letter red (stop).

★ Physically guide the student's hand.

★ Do movement activities that reinforce awareness of left and right (like Simon Says and the Hokey Pokey).

★ Use flexible and ongoing practice using a multimodal approach. (Have the students practice in a variety of places using different materials, including magnetic letters, Wikki Stix, Magna Doodle, chalk, crayon on a screen, writing on a whiteboard or in the air, and so on.)

★ Use fabric glue to provide 3-D tactile dots on a page to indicate where writing starts (green dot) and where to stop (red dot).

★ Have students sort letters by structure and features (circles, lines, and so on).

★ Provide an individual number line or alphabet strip for students' easy reference.

★ Have students trace over dots to form letters and numbers.

★ Use sandpaper letters, and write in salt or with sand.

★ Talk through letter formation; recording these directions in your own voice as opposed to purchasing font software, is very meaningful to students.

★ Use screen spelling. (Purchase three to four yards of medium mesh aluminum screen at the hardware store. With a marker and a yardstick, make 9-inch × 12-inch grids, and then cut out the individual screens. Cover the prickly edges with masking tape or duct tape. Students place the screen on their desks with a sheet of paper on top of the screen. This produces a raised surface. Using a crayon, the students practice making letters, words, and so on. Students can then trace the raised letters with their eyes open or closed and then write the word in the air. This tactile experience enhances letter and word study and reduces letter reversals.)

What Really Matters for Struggling Early Readers

There are many causes for underachievement in reading. This book does not focus on the obstacles, labels, or deficits. Instead, it provides strategies to build success and increase achievement for all. Following are some basic principles to keep in mind in designing a success-oriented literacy program.

What really matters to struggling students includes:

- ★ Classroom organization (flexible grouping, access to a variety of books and writing materials, classroom routines, and literacy centers, for example)
- ★ Providing choices, such as different genres, different topics, and narrative and informational texts
- ★ Providing direct instruction in phonemic awareness and phonics, including word study instruction and decoding support
- ★ Explicit and strategic instruction in text comprehension
- ★ Responding to reading with different processes and purposes
- ★ Assessment that is ongoing, formative, performance-based, and student-centered
- ★ Fluency so students get beyond "barking at print"

Final Thoughts

It is important to focus on early intervention skills for students to be successful in emergent literacy and close the gap as they move from learning to read to reading to learn. High-quality instruction needs to be integrated within a balanced literacy program that concentrates on monitoring student progress and targeting skill gaps. The next chapter provides specific strategies for planning and scaffolding instruction for vocabulary learning.

4. Vocabulary Strategies: Helping Students Become Word Wise

Vocabulary development is critical to literacy achievement. One of the most persistent findings in reading research is that the extent of students' vocabulary knowledge relates directly to their ability to comprehend and to their overall reading success (Baumann, Kame'enui, & Ash, 2003). Vocabulary knowledge is also one of the best predictors of verbal ability (Jensen, 1980). It is important to note that people possess four distinct and overlapping vocabularies: (1) listening, (2) reading (receptive language), (3) speaking, and (4) writing (expressive language). Young students have much larger listening and speaking vocabularies than reading and writing vocabularies. Helping students further develop their vocabularies is a challenge for educators.

Teachers need a variety of "fab vocab" strategies that are active, engaging ways to expand the listening and speaking vocabulary of their students. These techniques are hands-on, practical, and effective—well suited to busy classroom literacy programs. As students increase their vocabularies, they boost their reading comprehension and strengthen their ability to tackle informational text. In developing and enhancing your program for word learning, keep in mind that the program of instruction you create for students should be personal, active, flexible, and strategic.

Consider the following questions as you prepare to plan your vocabulary instruction.

- ★ What do I believe about the importance of word learning?
- ★ Do I have a narrow- or broad-based view of integrating vocabulary instruction throughout the curriculum?
- ★ When I introduce new words, do I always follow the same procedure?
- ★ In my classroom, who does the most talking about new words?

★ How do I create a "wonder of words"? Do I make work involving words personal, active, multisensory, flexible, and strategic?

These fundamental questions about word study and vocabulary development are an important reflection tool to use before embarking on developing or modifying your vocabulary program. It is important to articulate what is as a first step before it's possible to effectively determine what could be.

Promoting Vocabulary Acquisition and Use

Teachers must communicate the importance of word learning and acquiring a strong vocabulary. Researchers concur that students need to add 2,000 to 3,500 vocabulary words per year to their reading vocabularies to support literacy development (Anderson & Nagy, 1992; Anglin, Miller, & Wakefield, 1993; Beck & McKeown, 1983; White, Graves, & Slater, 1990), and this must be done in only 180 instructional days. Therefore, teachers need to offer explicit and daily vocabulary instruction throughout the subject areas, not just as isolated lessons. They must facilitate both *direct* and *indirect* vocabulary acquisition.

Struggling students need particular attention with explicit vocabulary instruction because vocabulary difficulty strongly influences the readability of texts (Klare, 1984). Isabel Beck and Margaret McKeown (1983) concur that teaching the vocabulary of a selection can improve students' comprehension of that selection. Decades of research have consistently confirmed the relationship among vocabulary knowledge, reading comprehension, and academic success (Baumann et al., 2003). The importance of vocabulary knowledge as a principle contributor to comprehension is further supported by the research of Peter Freebody and Richard C. Anderson (1983), Frederick B. Davis (1972), P. David Pearson and colleagues (2007), and Judith N. Thelen (1986).

It is important to focus on word meaning. When does a student truly know a word? For teachers, the dilemma is often in vocabulary versus spelling. Knowing a word by sight and sound and being able to recite the dictionary definition are not the same as being able to make meaning of the word, using it in various contexts, and understanding it beyond the text (Miller & Gildea, 1987).

When deciding on which words to teach, make vocabulary choices by asking:

★ Is the word critical to making meaning of the text or story?
★ Is the word useful to the student beyond the text in his or her life?

If the answer is yes, then teach it!

Promoting Word Consciousness

Unfortunately, research documents that students starting school with smaller vocabularies are at a distinct academic deficit that most of them never overcome

(Hart & Risley, 1995, 2003). Nell Duke (2004) emphasizes the vital importance of word awareness with students and found that the relationship between vocabulary and comprehension is unparalleled in importance in any literacy program. Many teachers see vocabulary as necessary for better reading and understand the long-term effect that word knowledge has on learning, achievement, thinking skills, and communication (Bromley, 2002; Watts, 1995). Vocabulary knowledge is also a key contributor to fluency. In fact, 80 percent of fluency is related to vocabulary recognition and pronunciation (Fuchs, Fuchs, Hosp, & Jenkins, 2001). Therefore, an extensive vocabulary helps students read fluently, comprehend what they read, and be able to discuss what they have read and learned. Given the importance of vocabulary, teachers need to be strategic as well as enthusiastic about promoting the wonder of words and word consciousness.

Make Word Learning Visible

Teach your students to be word detectives, and help them discover a sense of wonder in gathering new words for their own personal word banks. Make word learning visible by listing core vocabulary on the walls. There should be no escape from learning! In fact, make a game out of it. For example, each time you use an identified key vocabulary word in the word bank, or students encounter a key vocabulary word in their reading, they tally it and celebrate their word discoveries.

Make Words Sparkle

If you make words sparkle, students will want to catch them! Have students select key words of the week. These words should be new, interesting, and challenging. See if they can use the words in new ways, and let them earn points for their unique contributions. For example, they can illustrate words and make word cards that list synonyms and antonyms and feature the word in a sentence. Students can keep a vocabulary log of these new and exciting words and use them in writing and speaking. Make these words multidimensional: create word mobiles that hang in the classroom. Another way to help with retention and comprehension for visual learners is to sketch the meaning of a word and make a set of flash cards with the graphic symbols for new words.

For the kinesthetic learner, ask students to act out the meanings of new words during word theater. Write individual words on index cards and place them in a box. One student selects a card and acts it out for a small group of students who try to guess what the word is. Whoever guesses the word correctly then takes a turn to act out a new word.

Foster Word Awareness in Interesting Ways

To foster word awareness, give students a rich array of varied text types at different levels. This is essential for self-selection. When students come to a word they do not know, explain word meanings in a conversational way, rather than sounding like a dictionary. In other words, use the word in a sentence that the student can relate to. Here are some other strategies to easily integrate into your curriculum.

★ **Let me count the ways:** Students select a word chip and see if they can use the word in five different ways. This helps them make connections.

★ **Two for you:** Students work with a learning partner to select two word chips each to make a sample sentence that makes sense. For example, if a student chooses *sink* and *sand*, he or she might make a statement that uses both of the words in a meaningful way, such as, "If I drop *sand* in the water, I know it will *sink*." You might then ask students to create a visual to support their sentence.

★ **Three for me:** After mastering two word chips, have students try making sentences with three word chips. For example, if the words are *water*, *sand*, and *grains*, the student might make the sentence, "You can see grains of sand under the water in the ocean." Make sure that the words are appropriate to their age and developmental level.

★ **Go for it!:** After students have successfully made statements with two and three word-chip words, increase the complexity and level of difficulty. Have students make a sentence that uses all the word chips (fifteen to twenty vocabulary words). Ask them to share their sentences with the entire group. Encourage students to be silly and have fun with words.

★ **Fun with homographs:** Use games to teach the multiple meanings of homographs—words that are spelled the same but have different meanings and origins. An example of a homograph is *spell*.
    + Spell (to say letters)
    + Spell (to cast a magic spell)
    + Spell (a duration of time)

Activities like these provide language links and the opportunity for personal connections so that when students read, they will be more prepared to independently read text that includes the vocabulary words. These activities provide other contexts for the vocabulary words students will encounter. After students have mastered these techniques, give them words that are not in the text and ask them to make inferences. Invite them to retell the story or the passage that was read in their own words. When students say one of the key words, they can then make a pile of those word chips. With these activities, students are not just looking, listening, or reading passively.

Providing Rich Language Experiences

Encourage deep processing of word knowledge through engaging, multimodal approaches and a variety of exposures. A hands-on approach to vocabulary development is far more meaningful to students than the passive act of looking it up in the dictionary. In fact, dictionary use needs to be strategic and purposeful. A hands-on approach involves more learning done in less time so students are working smarter, not harder, by developing their psychomotor memory (Jensen, 2005).

Be sure to keep an ongoing list of key vocabulary prominently displayed. This can be a constantly evolving word wall that changes as your students' word knowledge grows and develops. If the words are visible and accessible to the students, they are more likely to see, think about, and use them.

Exposing students to a variety of texts on different topics and of different levels (called *wide reading*) enhances students' word knowledge; however, direct instruction in vocabulary influences achievement and comprehension more than any other factor (Baumann et al., 2003; Blachowicz & Fisher, 2000; Nagy, 1988; Stahl & Fairbanks, 1986). Vocabulary development is sustained over time through multiple exposures to words in different contexts. The following strategies help build exposure to vocabulary words in rich ways.

- ★ **Engaging teacher read-aloud:** Share your own love of words with your students and ignite and excite students to share theirs. Choose books with vibrant vocabulary and powerful language.
  - ✦ Print the key vocabulary words on index cards and pass them out to the students. If you have more students than word cards, ask students to work with partners. As you pass out the cards, pronounce each word so students recognize the sound of the word. As you read the story aloud, invite students to hold up their cards when they hear their words read. After students are familiar with the story from repeated reading, pause before the target word, and have the students guess which word would make sense in the sentence. This is a great way to use context clues for word meaning.
  - ✦ Use teacher read-aloud at least three times a day, and use it for narrative as well as informational text. While reading, demonstrate curiosity about words, and pause to wonder aloud and unpack fascinating words for students.
- ★ **Word wall whackers!:** Bring your traditional word wall to life by using flyswatters with the plastic webbing cut out in the center to make frames. Invite students to participate in a game of word wall whackers with statements such as the following.
  - ✦ Whack at least three nouns.
  - ✦ Whack a word that rhymes with _____.
  - ✦ Whack at least three verbs.
  - ✦ Whack a word that has more than three syllables.

+ Whack at least three adjectives.
+ Whack the word that means _____.
+ Whack a word that has a prefix.
+ Whack three words that were used in our story.
+ Whack a word that starts like your name.
+ Whack a word that means the same as _____.

★ **Vo-back-ulary:** Tape word cards on your students' backs. Then have them mix and mingle to some music, asking other students questions about their words. The other students provide clues to help students guess the word on their back. This is an active way to review and reinforce word meanings (Bromley, 2002).

★ **Word headbands:** This activity is similar to vo-back-ulary, but this time you write a "secret word" on a headband made out of stapled sentence strips that students are wearing (students can't see the words on their headbands). They mix and mingle, asking pertinent questions that will assist them in guessing what their secret word is. Some of the questions they can ask are—

+ What category does this word fit into?
+ What are some main characteristics of the word?

You can change the questions to meet the needs of the lesson. This activity increases student speaking and listening skills and provides a much-needed kinesthetic break in instruction.

★ **Quick draw:** See how quickly the students can sketch out a symbolic image of the word on the board for the rest of the class to guess. This can also be done with learning partners.

★ **Group related words:** Rather than teaching isolated words to memorize, teach words in related clusters that will enhance the meaning-making process. For example, have students group word together about emotions or feelings. Then have them discuss what it means to be frightened or delighted or terrified versus ecstatic. An extension activity would be to make posters that represent these groupings.

★ **Real-world words:** Have students become word detectives in their neighborhoods. The student needs to write down the word or take a picture of it, write down what it means, and note where she or he heard it or saw it.

★ **Examples and nonexamples:** Using words familiar to students, ask them to provide examples and nonexamples. This can be done with visual or verbal descriptions. They can work with partners and explain why something is a good example of a word or not. They are learning the important skill of comparing and contrasting and defending their ideas in writing.

For instance, for the term *mammal*, an example would be a cat, a dog, or a bear. A nonexample of a mammal would be a snake, a turtle, or a frog.

★ **Fill in the blanks:** Ask students to fill in the blanks in sentences with the key word missing before they are expected to construct sentences on their own. Be sure to point out how they can use context clues to help them. Share a word bank of the target words to choose from to help them succeed. Another variation is to create sentence frames with blanks to generate new words. For example, "Have a _____ day" helps generate multiple synonyms for the word *nice*.

Teaching Academic Vocabulary

An essential component of the standards-based curriculum movement is the focus on teaching academic vocabulary. Vocabulary development is embedded in the Common Core State Standards as well as state standards. Understanding words and phrases is essential to exploring key ideas and expanding knowledge in academic reading. Word learning is necessary for understanding text complexity.

It is important to address vocabulary within the context of meaningful reading. Give students opportunities to engage with words through authentic reading experiences. Some key points to remember for word learning (adapted from Allen, 1999) are:

★ **Connect to prior knowledge**—How much prior knowledge will the students have about this word and its related concepts?

★ **Share metacognitive knowledge**—Which words are most important to understanding the meaning of the text?

★ **Actively engage students in a variety of ways**—What strategies could I utilize to help students integrate the concept (and related words) into their lives?

★ **Don't fall into the "preteaching vocabulary" trap every time**—Is the concept significant enough to require preteaching?
  ✦ Do the students actually need to know this word or phrase to do the task?
  ✦ Could they guess it from context?
  ✦ Can this word or phrase be used productively within this lesson?

★ **Apply strategies across the curriculum**—How can I make repeated exposures to the word or concept productive and enjoyable? Integrate and explicitly teach content across the content areas so that students have an understanding of academic vocabulary specific to the subject matter.

★ **Teach strategies for independence**—How can students figure out words on their own? Use context clues (to guess meaning), vocabulary journals (to keep track of learned words), and structural analysis (to look at word structure or word parts that are known to determine the meaning of unfamiliar words).

★ **Share the benefits of word learning, citing real-life examples**—Why do students need to increase their vocabularies, and when will they use this knowledge?

Discovering the Wonder of Words

Deep word study does not happen by chance. Students need multiple exposures to words in various contexts throughout the instructional day to achieve mastery. The following strategies are engaging ways to enrich students' vocabulary knowledge and can be integrated throughout the curriculum and content areas.

★ **Word chains:** This vocabulary-linking activity is fast-paced and provides an active review of previously taught words. Start with ten to twelve cards that define one word on one side and another word on the other.

The first student says, "I have [word from the front of the card]. Who has a word that means [definition from the back of the card]?" Students then read their cards. If they have the word that matches the definition, they stand and shout, "I have [word that matches the definition]! Who has a word that means [definition from the back of their card]?" The cycle continues until the last student shares his or her definition.

★ **Anticipation guide:** Provide students with a list of words and definitions, some of which are accurate and some that are not. Students predict whether they agree or disagree with the words and definitions. Discuss this using context clues and word clues, such as prefixes, suffixes, root words, and so on. Revisit the anticipation guide after reading the text to see if students want to change any of their previous predictions based on the new knowledge they have gained because of the lesson.

★ **Vocabulary bingo:** Prepare bingo cards with randomly mixed vocabulary words written in each of the boxes. Distribute bingo cards to the class. You can either call out definitions of various words and students place a marker on or cross out the corresponding word, or you can read a cloze sentence— one with the key word omitted. Students shout out the appropriate word that fits and mark it on their board.

★ **Concept maps:** Have students place a key vocabulary word in the center of a piece of chart paper and then create a word web of synonyms for the key word. This is best done with learning partners or in small groups. Display the word maps around the room for reinforcement.

★ **Interview a word:** In this activity, students become the words. Select key words and divide the class into teams. Have the students work together to become the word by thinking about various aspects of the word as well as the meaning and function of the word (Bromley, 2002). Give each team a list of interview questions for the students to answer about their word. The teams then interview each other, and the class guesses the target word. For example, the word is *proud*. Students might ask the following questions. The replies are in parentheses.

+ Can you tell us a little bit about yourself? (*People think of me as snobby.*)
+ Who are your relatives? (*Vain, conceited*)
+ What is your purpose? (*I am an adjective.*)
+ What do you like? (*Myself*)
+ What don't you like? (*Humble people*)

★ **"Get the gist" with gestures:** Students will remember words better if you use gestures to explain them; it is all in the hands! This is a particularly useful technique for English learners. As you go over each word, explain it and add a gesture using your hands, face, or head. Have the students mirror your actions and repeat after you.

★ **Finger play:** This is a quick and engaging way to review and reinforce vocabulary for tactile and kinesthetic learners. Have students work in pairs. One student reads one of the key vocabulary words, and the other student draws a representation of the word in the air with his or her finger. Who needs paper?

★ **Break the bank:** Create a "vocabulary vault" that can be an easily accessed, such as a basket or bowl, containing the words of the week. A student or the teacher draws a word from the bank, and the class either guesses the word (by the definition) or defines the word. This can be done throughout the day as a brain break and to review key vocabulary words.

★ **Word windowpane:** Have students create a word windowpane by folding a sheet of paper into fourths. Write one of the following categories in each quadrant.

+ Words that make noise
+ Words that mean action
+ Words that confuse me
+ Words that paint a picture
+ Words that make me laugh
+ Words that ask questions
+ Words that describe
+ Words that have more than three syllables

Students fill up their individual word windowpane with words of their own choosing. Have them keep the windowpanes as word banks to study for a test or to use when they are writing stories or essays.

★ **Wondering about words:** Give students paper with four columns on it. Label the columns—

 i. Words I don't know
 ii. Words I have seen before but am not sure of
 iii. Words I think I know
 iv. Words I know

Provide key vocabulary words for the lesson before the students do their reading of the text. This way they are able to identify words that are known and words that they need to find out more about. This is an excellent needs-assessment tool so you realize the words to focus instruction on.

★ **Buried words:** Create a "word graveyard" bulletin board in your classroom. Have the students create tombstones for words that are overused, boring, or vague. This is a way for students to talk about words and the meanings they convey. Model the activity for them. For example, if the word *said* is in the word graveyard, have students come up with similar words that convey that meaning in a more vibrant way (such as *exclaimed*, *shouted*, and *proclaimed*).

★ **Words that grow:** Draw the outline of a tree with many branches and an empty box beneath the ground to represent the root word. Students think of as many examples as possible of words that have the root word written in the box. They then write the words on the branches of the tree. For example, *spect* is the root word, and branches could include *spectator*, *inspect*, *respect*, and *spectacle*.

★ **Rhyme, rhythm, rap:** Have the students create rhymes, rhythms, and raps for words and their definitions. This is a powerful memory tool for the musical students in your class and increases retention for everyone.

★ **Mystery word bags:** In a bag, place objects or pictures representing key concepts and vocabulary from the text or unit the students are studying. Have students work with learning partners to examine the contents of the bag and make their best guesses as to what the vocabulary words are based on the contents of the bag. After they have mastered this strategy, have the students create word bags for each other. For example, a bag might contain a photo of an astronaut on the moon, a book cover image for *The Prince of Tides*, a Fig Newton cookie wrapper, and a photo of water flowing from a sink. These items symbolize the concept of gravity.

★ **Word weaving:** Present a list of key words on the board or on a chart. The list should include both familiar and unfamiliar words. Discuss the meaning of the new words. Students then work with partners or in small groups to create sentences that include as many of the new words as possible. Record sentences on the board, and underline the target words.

Using the context clues of the text, students compare their original sentence to the meaning of the word as revealed by the text. They then have the opportunity to revise their original sentence based on the actual meaning of the word. They record their final sentences in their learning logs.

★ **Sort it out:** This version of a semantic sort activity is a hands-on approach to word study. Students sort words into categories that they create and then attach a label to them. Select a list of key words to introduce in a text or unit. Distribute these words to the class. Students work with partners, cutting up the words to create word chips that they can manipulate and sort. Before reading the passage, ask students to group the words in a way that makes sense to them. Students then share the labels of the categories that they have sorted the words into. Ask students to then predict what will happen in the story based on the words and how they have sorted them. Ask the students to read the text, pausing to reflect during their reading. Then ask them to re-sort the words based on the meaning of the passage. After reading the passage, they should write their final sorted words in their word study notebooks for discussion.

Final Thoughts

Engaging students in active wordplay activities is a critical part of literacy programs and boosts written and spoken vocabulary skills. A hands-on, minds-on approach to words promotes student interest and curiosity about words. Providing opportunities in your literacy program for students to play with words is not only vital to enhance their vocabulary but also needed to increase text comprehension.

The next chapter explores using graphic organizers to help students organize their thoughts as they read. You can use these tools and techniques to help with students' vocabulary development and word work as well.

5 Graphic Organizers: Making Thinking Visible

Are you looking for ways to help students with their retention in reading, improve their writing process, and enhance their organizational skills? Graphic organizers, such as diagrams, concept maps, word webs, frames, charts, and clusters, illustrate concepts and relationships between ideas in a text. Students use these visual representations of knowledge to structure information (Bromley, DeVitis, & Modlo, 1999). Graphic organizers also help students stay focused on content material and can reinforce previously learned material. They encourage higher-level thinking skills and active thinking. Multiple studies have validated that graphic organizers do indeed increase comprehension (Darch, Carnine, & Kame'enui, 1986; Horton, Lovitt, & Bergerud, 1990; Marzano et al., 2001).

Graphic organizers help students who struggle with writing activities organize their ideas. Students who find note taking challenging, whether they are taking notes on the main idea and details from a text or notes from a class discussion or lesson, get support from graphic organizers. Graphic organizers are important visual learning tools for teachers as well. Teachers can use them to help make new ideas easier to understand and learn (Meyen, Vergason, & Whelan, 1996). This chapter focuses on using graphic organizers as an engaging, research-based method to improve students' conceptual understanding and comprehension.

The Power of Graphic Organizers to Structure Thinking

Having a way to organize ideas, facts, and concepts into a visual learning tool helps students (Billmeyer & Barton, 2002):

- ★ Think categorically
- ★ Actively manipulate information to see connections and relationships between concepts
- ★ Reinforce their knowledge of text structures

★ Retain information by making associations between ideas from various sources
★ Demonstrate how concepts are linked to prior knowledge to enhance comprehension and retention
★ Evaluate information to determine what is most important
★ Generate mental images to extend and apply ideas
★ Depict relationships among facts and concepts
★ Store and retrieve information in a visual way
★ Become ready for college and career (where visual representations are used frequently)
★ Facilitate thinking, writing, summarizing, and discussing
★ Focus on the relationship of information as opposed to the mere memorization and recitation of facts
★ Be engaged in cooperative learning structures
★ Take notes and link new information to what they already know
★ Review information from previous learning while also learning new information

In addition, graphic organizers enhance the learning outcomes of students with many different learning styles.

★ **Verbal-linguistic learners:** When information is presented auditorily through discussions and think-alouds, graphic organizers allow verbal-linguistic learners to record what they hear as images.
★ **Logical-mathematical learners:** Students use logic skills to organize concepts and information graphically, make connections, and categorize and classify data.
★ **Visual-spatial learners:** These students tend to think in pictures and create images in their minds to retain and process information. Charts and diagrams and other visual representations are tools to boost their comprehension and enhance the meaning-making process.

Types of Graphic Organizers

David Ausubel (1963) concluded that the manner and style in which ideas and information are represented can influence learning. Matching the appropriate organizer with the content of the lesson can help students form relationships between what has been taught and new concepts. Graphic organizers can be used in varied ways. The student's age, ability level, grade level, and learning styles; the content area; the concept to be learned; and the desired outcomes of the lesson all determine the format and function of the organizer chosen.

Typical types of graphic organizers include:

Comparative Organizers

These tools help students compare and contrast two ideas or concepts according to their features. Examples of comparative organizers are a Venn diagram and a compare/contrast matrix.

Descriptive or Thematic Maps

These tools work well for displaying general information and hierarchical information (see figures 5.1 and 5.2).

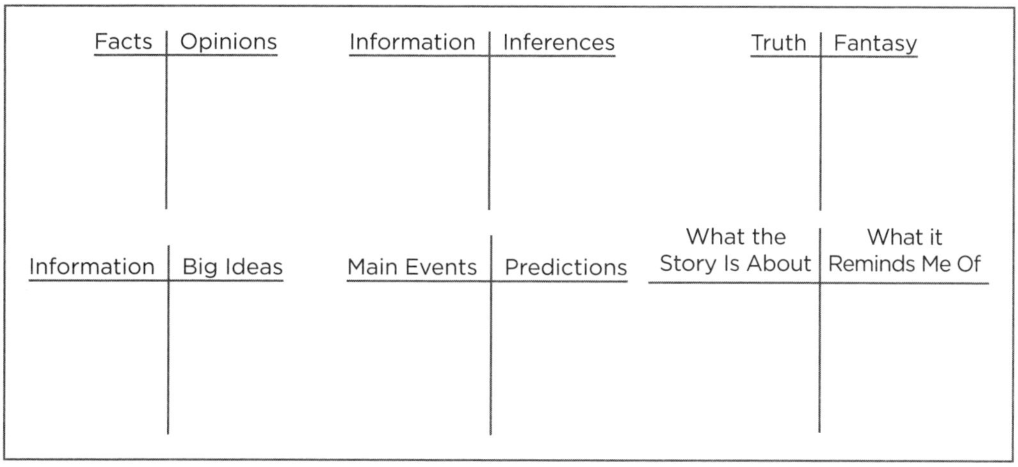

Facts	Opinions		Information	Inferences		Truth	Fantasy
Information	Big Ideas		Main Events	Predictions		What the Story Is About	What it Reminds Me Of

Figure 5.1: T-Charts.

*Visit **go.SolutionTree.com/literacy** for a free reproducible version of this figure.*

Describe the word:	Synonym:
_____	_____
_____	
_____	
_____	

Vocabulary word:

Antonym:	Draw a picture or write a sentence:
_____	

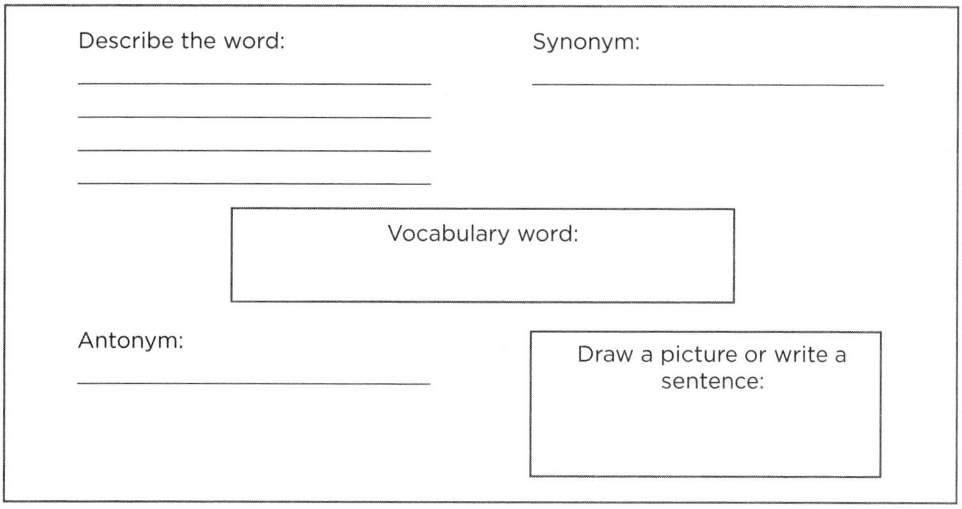

Figure 5.2: Vocabulary map.

*Visit **go.SolutionTree.com/literacy** for a free reproducible version of this figure.*

Problem and Solution Maps

With these tools, the problem is on one line and the possible solutions are connected in an organized pattern (see figure 5.3). This is useful when the information contains cause-and-effect problems and solutions.

Problem–Solution Outlines

These tools help students compare and generate various solutions to a central problem (see figure 5.4).

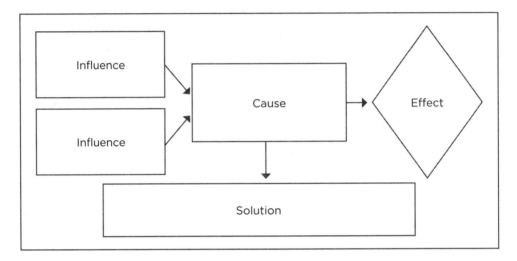

Figure 5.3: Problem and solution map.

*Visit **go.SolutionTree.com/literacy** for a free reproducible version of this figure.*

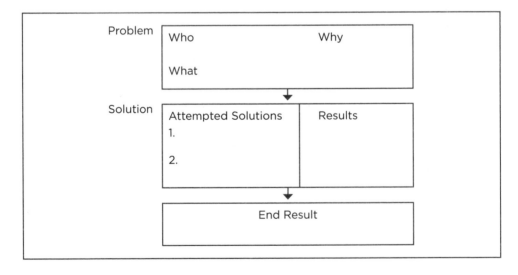

Figure 5.4: Problem-solution outline.

*Visit **go.SolutionTree.com/literacy** for a free reproducible version of this figure.*

Continuum Scales

These are effective tools for organizing information along a progression from less to more, low to high, or few to many.

Cyclical Organizers

These tools display a series of recurring events and do not have a beginning or end—for example, a cycle map or a series-of-events chain (see figure 5.5).

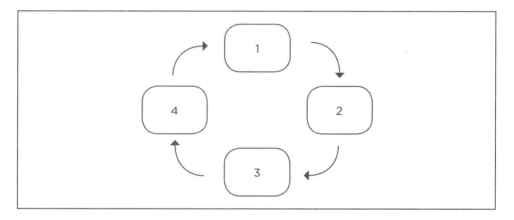

Figure 5.5: Cycle map.

*Visit **go.SolutionTree.com/literacy** for a free reproducible version of this figure.*

Fishbone Maps

For these tools, the central idea is the body of the fish, and the bones represent evidence or solutions organized around the central theme (see figure 5.6). For example, if a central storyline is the fish, then the who, what, where, when, and why are the bones of the fish. A fishbone map might also be useful for lessons in which cause-effect relationships are more complex and not redundant.

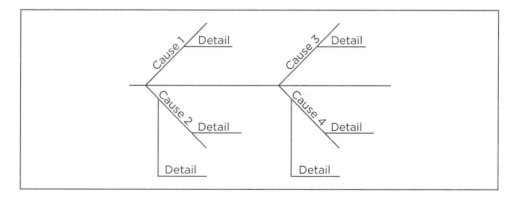

Figure 5.6: Fishbone map.

*Visit **go.SolutionTree.com/literacy** for a free reproducible version of this figure.*

Hierarchical Organizers

These tools display main ideas and supportive details in order, reflecting subordinate or superordinate concepts as a network tree (see figures 5.7 and 5.8).

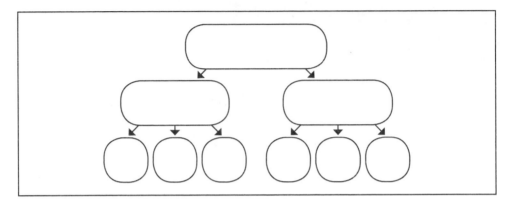

Figure 5.7: Network tree.

*Visit **go.SolutionTree.com/literacy** for a free reproducible version of this figure.*

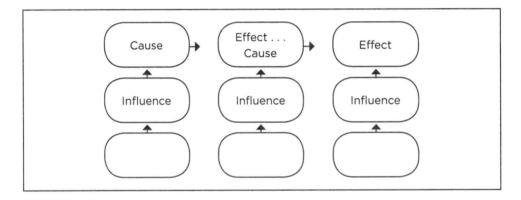

Figure 5.8: Cause-and-effect chart.

*Visit **go.SolutionTree.com/literacy** for a free reproducible version of this figure.*

K-W-L Chart

This tool shows what students know, what they want to know, and what they have learned. Students brainstorm responses independently, with partners, or in small groups before and after the lesson.

Sequential Organizers

These tools, such as a sequence map and a sequence episodic map, depict a series of steps in chronological order (see figure 5.9).

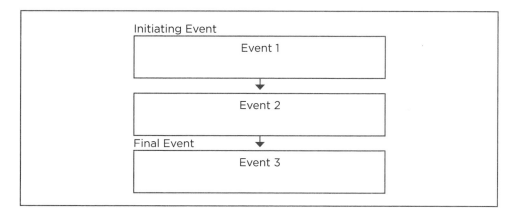

Figure 5.9: Sequential organizer.

*Visit **go.SolutionTree.com/literacy** for a free reproducible version of this figure.*

Diagrams

These visuals depict actual objects, systems, and events in science, social studies, or other content areas.

Conceptual Organizers

These tools, such as a spider map (see figure 5.10), expand upon a central idea with supporting facts, evidence, qualities, or characteristics around a central topic or idea. This tool is useful when the main idea or theme does not fit into a hierarchy.

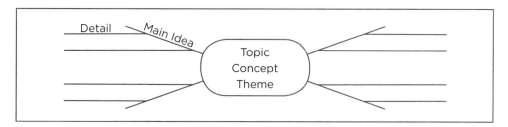

Figure 5.10: Spider map.

*Visit **go.SolutionTree.com/literacy** for a free reproducible version of this figure.*

How to Choose a Graphic Organizer

The different types of graphic organizers have many uses in instruction. For example, if you want to show a sequence or series of events, you would probably select a cycle diagram or a sequential organizer to display that information. Selecting the appropriate organizer can be the key to helping students make connections between previously acquired knowledge and new ideas.

You can use graphic organizers before, during, and after the lesson as an instructional tool to support learning in the following ways.

- ★ As a study aid
- ★ For brainstorming
- ★ To summarize
- ★ To activate prior knowledge
- ★ To create a story map of key events
- ★ To make predictions
- ★ As a tool for reflection
- ★ To describe main ideas, details, and patterns

Although reading is the most common and studied subject in which to apply graphic organizers in the curriculum, they can also be used to enhance comprehension in science, social studies, mathematics, language arts, and other subject areas. The benefits of using graphic organizers in other content areas are well documented (Bulgren, Schumaker, & Deshler, 1988; Darch et al., 1986; Willerman & MacHarg, 1991).

Research (Baxendell, 2003) has identified three key factors to consider for successful implementation of graphic organizers in the classroom. These key factors are referred to as the 3Cs of using graphic organizers: *consistent*, *coherent*, and *creative*.

Being consistent means selecting a standard set of graphic organizers for students to use. Once they have mastered that certain set of structures, they can branch out on their own. Establishing clear procedures and routines for implementing them in the classroom is also necessary.

When using graphic organizers in the classroom, ask yourself, "How coherent are these structures? Do they enhance or detract from the lesson?" Set the students up for success by presenting clear labels for the relationship between concepts in graphic organizers. Limit the number of ideas and organizers you cover. Strive for lesson mastery first. Minimize distractions and clearly explain the process and products desired to students before they engage in independent practice.

Keep creativity flourishing throughout the lesson. Incorporate graphic organizers for a quick review or have students create them for homework to extend learning. Invite learners to add symbolic summaries or illustrations to enhance their organizers. Utilize collaborative learning teams, partners, or cooperative learning groups to work together to create organizers and share what students have learned.

Steps for Implementing Graphic Organizers

If you want to introduce graphic organizers to your students and have them develop their own, use the following steps as a framework.

1. Discuss the purpose of and process for using graphic organizers, and demonstrate with a basic overview. Show students the various types of organizers and their specific uses and benefits.
2. Analyze the information to be taught and highlight key words and phrases to model this step for students.
3. Model identifying the relationship between concepts and facts to determine the most appropriate organizer to use, and model it for instruction.

   Remember, using multiple organizers all at once can be quite confusing to the struggling reader, so keep it simple. Think about the purpose of the organizer (is it for presenting new information or a guide for taking notes, for example?).
   + For teacher modeling, it should be simple and uncluttered and have a large font.
   + Leave empty spaces for student participation.
   + Use color to highlight key components.
   + Make sure that there is adequate space for writing key information when taking notes.
4. Conduct a think-aloud lesson, completing the graphic organizer on the board as you go.
5. Prepare the graphic organizer (whole first, then partial and blank, so students see the progression). Students should have a printed model of the graphic organizer so that they can complete it while you are demonstrating.
6. Add pictures, symbols, or images to capture students' attention and to make the concepts you are teaching more obvious.
7. Place students in cooperative groups so that they can work with learning partners to complete the organizer, adding their own ideas. Provide support as needed.
8. Once the students have mastered using the organizers in pairs, have them work independently to complete the graphic organizer.

Provide multiple opportunities for practicing each type of organizer before moving on to a new type. Students need to rehearse the new ways of structuring information.

Final Thoughts

Graphic organizers can be powerful tools for teachers and students for organizing content and ideas. They provide frames for students to identify facts and ideas, organize information, and make connections within a passage or story. Graphic organizers' use of visual and spatial modalities facilitates student comprehension of content and reinforces what is taught in the classroom. By creating a visual summary, graphic organizers help students see relationships and connections between facts and information they are learning. These learning tools engage a wide variety of learners, including struggling readers, by integrating text and visual imagery. Graphic organizers allow students to develop higher-level thinking skills, not merely acquire content. Students are learning new patterns for organizing their thoughts and ideas and for processing, communicating, and summarizing and synthesizing information.

6 Content Strategies: Navigating Informational Text

This chapter focuses on specific strategies to help students better comprehend informational texts. Making content comprehensible across the curriculum for struggling readers can be a daunting task. Sandra McCormick (2007) states that expository texts, also known as informational texts (textbooks, journal articles, lab procedures, and government documents, for example), are more difficult to comprehend than narrative texts (such as realistic and historical fiction, myths, fairy tales, plays, and legends). According to William Twining (1991), there are five reasons for this lack of reading comprehension.

1. Failure to understand a word
2. Failure to understand a sentence
3. Failure to understand how sentences relate to one another
4. Failure to understand how the information fits together in a meaningful way (organization of text)
5. Lack of interest or concentration

Students first learn to read narrative, story-like text structures with a beginning, middle, and end sequence. Then there is a shift to more expository, informational text structures, especially with the implementation of the Common Core State Standards. Increased emphasis on reading expository texts means learning and applying strategies for comprehending these texts is critical. Leigh Hall (2005) states that failure to comprehend informational text may result in a "ripple effect" across the curriculum, including an inability to learn the required course content, a lack of understanding of academic vocabulary, an inability to successfully pass tests, decreased self-confidence, and even behavioral problems. Therefore, for students to be successful in today's information age, they need to be able to gain meaning from a variety of texts (Mason, Meadan, Hedin, & Corso, 2006; Montelongo & Hernandez, 2007).

The research concludes that successful strategies can be taught (Collins, 1996; Farstrup & Samuels, 2002; Tovani, 2011) to make informational texts more comprehensible for struggling students. Instruction needs to be explicit and built upon students' background knowledge. In addition, features of texts as well as text structures need to be explicitly taught. This chapter focuses on practical strategies for success to help struggling readers become purposeful, active readers who succeed in comprehending expository texts.

Challenges of Informational Text

Struggling students face many challenges with comprehending informational text. The structures of expository text are quite different than the predictable narrative story structures that students have been exposed to in the early primary grades. In today's digital world, students need the essential tools to access informational text as an essential 21st century skill. Struggling readers are also often underprepared for monitoring their understanding of text and are often characterized as "passive readers" (Gajria, Jitendra, Sood, & Sacks, 2007).

Common problems that students have when encountering expository texts include:

* Lack of background knowledge
* Challenges with understanding content-area vocabulary
* Unfamiliarity with text structures and features

Additionally, McCormick (2007) lists six factors that interfere with struggling students' comprehension of informational text: (1) text structure, (2) new information, (3) academic vocabulary, (4) readability level of text, (5) abstract ideas and concepts, and (6) retention of information read. Hall (2005) and Joyce Jennings, JoAnne Caldwell, and Janet Lerner (2006) indicate that expository texts can be challenging for struggling readers because they contain content-specific vocabulary with more technical terms; are less personal, more concept dense, and require more background knowledge; and are often at students' frustration level of readability.

Strategies for Tackling Informational Text

Teachers need to consider new compensatory strategies to help students who are struggling with informational texts in order to build on their natural curiosity. Nell Duke (2004) suggests that teachers start at the primary level to provide access to and success with informational text, before intermediate or secondary grades. She suggests the following items.

* Increase students' access to informational texts—build your classroom library.
* Increase the instructional time spent during the day with informational text activities, including teacher read-aloud.
* Explicitly teach comprehension strategies, including academic vocabulary and text structures.

★ Increase opportunities for students to use informational texts throughout the content areas for real purposes.

In making comprehension instruction explicit, do not assume that students know when and why they should use particular strategies. Tell them what strategies to use and why and how to use them through teacher modeling and guidance. The steps for making instruction explicit include:

★ **Direct description and explanation**—Describing why the strategy helps them make meaning and when to use it

★ **Modeling**—Demonstrating how to apply the strategy by using think-aloud techniques during shared reading and teacher read-aloud

★ **Guided practice**—Guiding learning partners on how and when to use the strategies with real text examples

★ **Application**—Encouraging independence as the teacher provides additional scaffolded practice so that the students can succeed independently

Extensive research supports teaching strategies to struggling readers and the difference it makes for improved comprehension (National Reading Panel, 2000; Pressley, 2000). The following are basic strategies to enhance comprehension for struggling readers according to Kathy Jongsma (2001).

★ **Ask:** Does it make sense?

★ **Justify:** Why does it make or not make sense?

★ **Talk:** Talk and use thinking aloud to model strategies to students. Have students talk as they work with a learning partner.

★ **Predict:** Have students predict what will happen next or what the chapter will be about.

★ **Wait:** Allow adequate think time for students to respond.

Prereading Strategies

Comprehension instruction needs to be front-loaded with activities that are initiated before reading the text (McCormick, 2007). The following strategies are designed to help your students understand what they are about to read.

★ Identifying what counts as prereading

★ Exploring relevant background knowledge

★ Setting a purpose for the reading

★ Previewing the text to get a sense of the content and structure

★ Putting the ideas in context

★ Examining comprehension tips before reading

These instructional techniques help activate students' learning and familiarize them with the language, academic vocabulary, key concepts, and structures of expository texts. P. David Pearson (2003) supports these strategies and affirms the importance of teaching using informational texts because it helps students build the skills needed to be successful in school, at work, and in the community. The following are other reasons to engage in prereading activities.

★ They engage and motivate students.

★ They activate prior knowledge that is pertinent to text.

★ They encourage text preview so students get the gist of the structure and content of the reading.

★ They provide an opportunity to probe into unknown topics or themes.

★ They build student confidence and competence in exploring complex text.

Although prereading strategies are important, students can become too dependent if teachers over-scaffold prior to reading. Here are some cautions to avoid overdoing prereading strategies.

★ The prereading activity should not take longer than the actual reading of the text.

★ Do not translate or paraphrase the text prior to reading so that the students feel as though they don't need to actually read the text.

★ Focus only on important and challenging big ideas of the text. If preview strategies emphasize aspects that do not contribute to meaning, they may distract students from overall comprehension of the main message.

★ Fostering independence is important for students; do not make the meaning for them. Give them tools to use to figure it out on their own.

★ Provide variety in prereading strategies; otherwise, students will become dependent on a particular approach and will miss the total learning experience when reading on their own.

Balance is important when utilizing prereading strategies. Plunging struggling students directly into a challenging text without a launchpad to their learning might have negative consequences for their comprehension.

When determining the extent of your prereading lesson, focus on the reader and the text and task. Provide direct instruction to the whole class with teacher modeling. For struggling students who need specific intervention, provide individual support and extended learning opportunities. First, consider the reader.

★ What is the discrepancy between the student's reading level and the readability level of the text?

★ Does the student have adequate background knowledge of the topic?

Next, consider the text and task.

★ What particular aspect of learning or what standard is being addressed?

★ Are you planning to reteach or reinforce concepts?

★ How much background has already been covered in class on the topic?

★ Is the text being used at the beginning of a unit or the end of a lesson?

The answers to these questions will help you design the appropriate prereading lesson.

Finally, read the text ahead of time to determine:

- ★ The purpose of the reading lesson
- ★ What students bring to the text
- ★ What prereading information to provide
- ★ How and when to provide prereading lessons to accomplish the purpose

Prereading lessons should be brief and in proportion to the length and duration of the assigned text. One of the purposes of prereading should be to stimulate students' creativity, engagement, and curiosity so that you foster a need to know and a desire to read the text.

Prereading lessons should also focus on academic vocabulary and concepts that students are not familiar with or likely to know or able to determine from context.

Techniques to Consider

You can implement the following prereading strategies with your students.

- ★ **ABC grid:** This is an excellent tool to activate background knowledge. Provide students with an ABC grid (with twenty-six spaces, one for each letter). Have them brainstorm words or phrases related to the topic that begin with each letter, writing the words in the appropriate spaces on the grid. Keep the grid handy throughout the reading so students can add key vocabulary as they go. Use this activity before, during, or after the reading. Students can work independently or with a partner.

- ★ **Admit ticket:** Use admit tickets before students read a selection of text. Ask them to respond to a specific prompt on an index card (as homework or a warm-up activity).

- ★ **Anticipation guide:** Prepare a list of statements that relate to the concepts the text will cover. Before reading a selection, students respond to several statements that challenge or support their preconceived ideas about key concepts in the text. Students read statements and then mark them with "agree" or "disagree." The key to a successful anticipation guide is creating a need to know they have to verify their opinions and beliefs. Statements should provoke discussions. Some suggestions include—
    + Statements that focus on the ideas in the reading you want students to think about more deeply
    + Statements that ask for students' reactions
    + Statements that can be verified in the reading to promote connecting to the text

Students can share their responses with a learning partner or do a corners activity where they "vote with their feet" and move to the corner that represents whether they agree or disagree. They then discuss their opinions with other students. This tool is important for student engagement because it sets the stage for learning. Students are able to tap into their background knowledge and share their opinions with others. It also creates a need to know so students listen or read more carefully to verify their responses on the anticipation guide.

Give students the opportunity to change their initial response based on the new information they have acquired after reading. Discuss with the students the correct response.

★ **Back to back:** Similar to an anticipation guide, this activity involves writing down several statements about a topic that students will be studying. It is a discussion strategy you can use to motivate your students to share their thoughts. Students work with learning partners, standing back to back with each other. This structure helps because they feel less reluctant to engage in a discussion and share their opinions with others.

For example, during a unit on the Olympics, to introduce the lesson, I shared this statement: "When someone is not good at sports, we should not let him or her play on our team." After I read the statement, I asked the students to work in partners, back to back, and respond with a thumbs-up or thumbs-down, depending on whether they agreed or disagreed. They turned to face each other and then gave a high-five if they responded the same or explained why they thought differently.

★ **Brainstorming:** Activating the brain before reading is an important process. Ask students to examine the title of the reading or the main concept and make a list, either independently or with learning partners, of everything that comes to their minds. They can create a concept map or other graphic organizer, and you can record these ideas on the board. This strategy allows students to recall and share their background knowledge about a topic and prepares them for making connections for the new knowledge they will gain from the text.

★ **Directed reading, thinking activity (DRTA):** In this activity, first activate prior knowledge through brainstorming and tell students to predict the content the text will cover. Then they think and ask questions. The next steps come while and after they read. Students revisit and revise their predictions based on the new knowledge they gained by reading the text.

★ **Expectation grids:** Before reading, students develop visual representations of their knowledge using a reading graphic organizer for fiction or expository texts. Students categorize their background knowledge to help them see the big picture about a topic. It creates a focus and purpose for reading, and students can use the grid as a note-taking guide.

Introduce this tool using a familiar topic—for example, pets.

+ Ask the students what details they would include if they were going to write about the topic—for example, type of pet, color of fur, training, and so on.

+ Ask the students to suggest details and point out the categories the details fall into—for example, species, appearance, temperament, and so on.

+ Ask the students to brainstorm other categories of information for the topic.

+ Using the text and major headings as a guide, students then identify general categories of information about the topic they would expect to find in the text.

+ Have the students record what they know about the topic on a grid (such as a concept map) using the various categories as headings. They can work independently or in pairs.

+ Have the students read a selection of text and fill in the categories with new information as they go along.

★ **I wonder why?:** Start the lesson with "I wonder why?" statements related to the text students are about to read to activate prior knowledge. By generating questions, students become more aware of whether they can answer the questions and if they understand what they're reading.

Model the strategy by first showing students the cover of the book. Think out loud, "I wonder what this story is going to be about?" Have students draw a quick sketch and then generate an "I wonder" question based on what they think might happen in the story. Share and discuss the questions with the students. As they become more adept at this process, their questions become more complex. Eventually, students create their own "I wonder why?" questions as they read the story or text and work with learning partners.

★ **Jigsaw:** This strategy can be used before or during the reading of a text. It is particularly effective for struggling readers because they are only responsible for a portion of the complete text, and they can utilize their speaking and listening skills as they share their summaries with others. The procedure is simple. Have students form smaller groups. The students then read their portions of the text and discuss with their expert group the two or three main ideas. They then form a home group with other students who read the other portions of the text and share the main ideas with them. In this way, the students hear about five to six topics other than their own.

★ **K-W-L:** A K-W-L chart is a three-column chart that includes the before, during, and after stages of the reading process (Ogle, 1986). This strategy provides a structure for students to share what they know about the topic, what they want to know (questions they have), and what they learned about the topic (they revisit the chart after they've read the text). This can be done independently, in pairs, or in a group while you moderate.

★ **List, group, label:** Identify key words and phrases from the text, and give them to the students. They work together with partners to sort the words, categorize them, and label the groups. Through sorting, students predict what the topic of the text will be. The students revisit the words after the reading and have another opportunity to rearrange them according to the new knowledge they gained from reading the text.

★ **Opinion/proof:** Using this two-column organizer, students present the central topic of the text they are about to read. In the left column, they make a list of their opinions about the concept. They read the text and then add their proof statements with citations from the text next to their opinions.

★ **Picture/question:** Students preview text to be read and look at the pictures and illustrations in the chapter. For each picture, chart, or graph, have students pose a question and then do careful reading to find out the answer.

★ **Possible sentences:** Provide key vocabulary to students (ten to twelve words directly from the text). The students work with partners or small groups to create possible sentences using the words to create anticipation about the ideas to be covered in the text. This allows students to think about how these words are related to each other. As they read, they will become word detectives looking for these words in the text and seeking out additional sentences with these words in context.

★ **Prewrite questions:** After skimming the text, students write questions that they have. As students read, they look for answers to these questions.

★ **Quick write:** After you identify the topic, ask students to write all that they know about the topic. They can also write questions they have about the topic. Students can share what they've written with a learning partner.

★ **SCAN strategy:** This strategy helps students become critical thinkers. The SCAN strategy gets your students to ask the right questions while they read (Salembier, 1999). Make a poster of the following steps for your bulletin board for all to see.

   + **S**urvey headings and turn them into what, why, or how questions.
   + **C**apture the captions and visuals. Read the visual clues in the chapter and try to understand the captions before proceeding. Then ask yourself what the clue or caption means.
   + **A**ttack boldfaced words. Focus on the highlighted or bolded words in the text and determine the meaning of each.
   + **N**ote and read the section questions.

It is important to read the questions at the end of the chapter *first* before reading because it gives a purpose for the reading and focuses struggling readers on what to look for in the text.

★ **Skimming and scanning:** The important skills of skimming and scanning are valuable for studying expository texts. They help students look for main ideas, structural clues, and specific facts, key words, or phrases. Having students skim and scan the text requires teacher modeling and practice. Direct the students to read and think about the title and focus on headings, the introductory paragraph, conclusions, and tables and charts before they read the text (Neufeld, 2005). Have students think about these questions: What is this chapter about? What are the main ideas of this text? What is the text structure, and how is it organized?

★ **SQ3R:** This is a useful prereading strategy where students are taught how to survey, question, read, recite, and review (Robinson, 1970). This technique helps students preview text to set a purpose for reading and encourages them to develop questions prior to reading the text. Before reading, students survey the text, skimming through it to look at pictures, headings, structures, and so on. Next, students pose questions they have or turn the headings into questions to look for. The students then complete the 3Rs: read to find answers to their questions, recite that information and write it down, and review the text.

★ **SQ4R:** Similar to the SQ3R strategy, SQ4R adds the reflect process after the reading to assist the students in making connections to the text.

★ **SQP2RS:** SQP2RS is a framework for reading expository texts. It includes the following steps (Vogt, 2000).

   i. **Surveying**—Students scan the text for one to two minutes.

  ii. **Questioning**—Students create questions that the text might answer (with or without teacher modeling and support).

 iii. **Predicting**—Students predict what they think they'll learn based on the questions they pose.

 iv. **Reading**—Students read the text, looking for answers to their questions and to validate or refute their predictions.

  v. **Responding**—Students answer questions and create new ones for the next portion of the text they will read.

 vi. **Summarizing**—In writing or verbally with a learning partner, students summarize the key concepts they learned from the text.

★ **Take a stand:** This can be used before or after reading a text. It allows students to express their opinions about a topic and then review and modify those opinions after the reading if they have changed. They also need to cite with support from the text why their opinions have changed. This helps reinforce the connection to text.

* **Venn diagram:** Students can use this graphic organizer as a preliminary comparison activity prior to reading a text. The students place similarities and differences about two different topics into two intersecting circles and then add information to the diagram as they read.

* **Word splash:** Select eight to fifteen key words or phrases from the text, including both familiar and more challenging words. Have students work with a learning partner to create sentences containing these words or phrases. Students then make predictions about the text. Allow time for students to revisit their sentences after reading to see how their predictions reflect the ideas of the passage.

Strategies During Reading

Encourage students to be actively engaged and connected to text throughout the reading experience. Paul Neufeld (2005) states that watching others model comprehension skills is the most effective way for students to acquire these skills. The following strategies will teach your students to monitor their own understanding of text and become more actively engaged. During reading, good readers:

* Actively read and respond to key points in the text
* Read sequentially, skimming over some parts
* Reread some sections for greater clarity
* Make notes as they read
* Focus on main ideas and supportive details
* Adjust predictions made during the prereading phase
* Make inferences and applications
* Connect the text to themselves and their own real-world experiences
* Paraphrase and synthesize information

To support students during reading, you should:

* Clearly set the purpose for the reading and model successful strategies
* Demonstrate think-aloud strategies to students to help them monitor their own reading
* Foster higher-level thinking skills through deeper questioning techniques
* Model strategies to make inferences and applications as students read
* Teach students how to summarize and synthesize as they read
* Ask students to pause throughout their reading to affirm or refute their earlier predictions and to answer the questions they posed

Techniques to Consider

The following are some strategies for during reading to implement with your students.

* **Act it out:** Pause during the text reading to have students act out what they are reading. This form of mind-body connection is a particularly powerful tool for kinesthetic learners to help them retain main concepts of the text.

* **Argument chart:** Students use a graphic organizer to take notes and record different points of view in the text. (See chapter 5 for different types of graphic organizers.)

* **Cause-effect chain:** This strategy helps students recognize and record cause-and-effect relationships. Students look at one item as a cause and others as effects and organize the information accordingly as they read.

* **Chunking:** Break the text into meaningful chunks to make the task of reading more manageable for struggling students so each chunk of text leads into the next.

* **Coding:** Create a list of "classroom codes" to use while reading. Make a chart with these displayed so that students remember the codes (Marcell, 2007). Codes may be symbols or letters of key features to assist students in interacting with text as they read. For example—

  ? = I don't understand.

  + = I already know this.

  A = I agree with this statement or idea.

  D = I disagree with this statement or idea.

  ! = Wow! This is an interesting point.

  V = This is a new vocabulary word.

  R = This reminds me of . . .

  Provide each student with sticky notes so they can code as they read. Have them share their coded sticky notes with a learning partner before having a whole-class discussion.

* **Do now:** This strategy is a quick technique to help students pause in their reading by asking for a quick response within a specific time (three to five minutes). You can write the question on the board or provide it verbally for a quick review.

* **Double-entry journals:** This strategy can be used in many different ways. Students make two columns on paper. Give key terms or main ideas of the text before reading, and have students write these in the left column. Students jot down details or facts they find in the reading in the right column. You can also do the reverse: you give students definitions or details, and they seek key terms or main ideas. These journals can also serve as a study guide for a test or quiz.

★ **Fix-up strategy:** What do you do when comprehension breaks down for struggling students while they read? Teaching students the fix-up strategy helps them deal with information that they do not understand. Students should reread, look ahead, stop, and relate information to what they already know, examining other resources and asking others for help when a breakdown occurs (Neufeld, 2005).

★ **Guided reading procedure (GRP):** This procedure was developed to assist and support underachieving readers in comprehending informational text (Manzo, 1975). Students first read the text and try to remember as many important facts as they can. They write down the ideas they remember and go back and look for ideas they may have missed to add to the list. Then they categorize or organize the information. This helps struggling readers read more critically and develop higher-level thinking skills as they read.

★ **Hierarchical summarization:** This strategy involves developing outlines while reading (McCormick, 2007). It helps with summarizing and note taking. The sequence for this structure is as follows.
   i. Students skim the first few pages of the assigned text, taking note of the headings.
   ii. Students use their notes to make an outline, using outline form (a capital A, B, C, and so on) for each section, adding headings with two to three lines drawn underneath for details.
   iii. Students read the section of text for the first subheading.
   iv. Students write a main-idea sentence next to the letter A in their own words. Underneath they write two to three details that support the main idea in their own words.
   v. Students continue reading sections one at a time and filling in the outline.
   vi. When the reading is complete, students review their summaries.
   vii. Students share their summaries in small groups.

★ **H map:** Students use this graphic organizer to help them compare two topics. This technique enables students to record and organize information from a given reading passage. It is similar to a Venn diagram, where students compare and contrast two different topics. Each topic appears on one side of the H-shaped organizer.

★ **Interrupted conversation:** Have students pair up and take turns reading a passage of informational text, paragraph by paragraph, and invite them to interrupt each other to discuss, question, or argue about the ideas in the text.

★ **Jigsaw:** This technique can also be used during the reading process. You assign each small group a section of the reading to summarize in their own words and share with others.

★ **Key sentences:** Using this strategy, students identify the most important sentence from the text. Younger students can write the sentence on a strip of paper. Older students can jot it down on a sticky note. Students share their statements with a learning partner and explain why they think it is the most important. They build their speaking and listening skills while they then explain their choices to a group of students. A way to extend this activity is for students to also choose their favorite sentences and indicate why. This strategy encourages students to develop close-reading skills, think critically, and look for main ideas, and it supports their thinking.

★ **Literature circles:** Literature circles are not limited to narrative literature only and can be used with multiple types of text. This independent reading activity prompts student-generated discussions on a chosen text. Students are actively engaged in speaking and listening to each other. They have an opportunity to share their thoughts, concerns, and understandings with each other. The group size is usually four to six students to maximize participation. Assign each member of the team a role to help guide the discussion.

  ✦ **Discussion director**—Develops four to six open-ended questions related to the text for the group to discuss

  ✦ **Connector**—Helps the group make connections between ideas in the text and the real world

  ✦ **Vocabulary enricher**—Finds four to six important words in the passage and defines them for the group (in context)

  ✦ **Summarizer**—Summarizes the key points and main ideas of the passage

★ **Open mind:** Have the students draw an open mind on a sheet of paper—the outline of a person's head, the outline of a brain, and so on. As they read, they fill their open minds with words, phrases, and images that they are thinking about and want to remember. After the reading, they can write about and explain their responses.

★ **Paired guided reading:** Students read with a learning partner and write notes to share with their partner at certain points during the reading.

★ **RAP:** In this strategy, students read a paragraph or section of text, ask what the main ideas are, and put the ideas down in their own words (paraphrase).

★ **Reading story map:** In this traditional reading comprehension activity, students receive a template to answer questions, find and define key vocabulary words, complete charts, or draw pictures of the passage's main concepts. These reading guides can be tailored to meet the individual needs of struggling students and can be adapted for differing kinds of texts. See figures 6.1 and 6.2 (page 78) for samples of these map activity sheets.

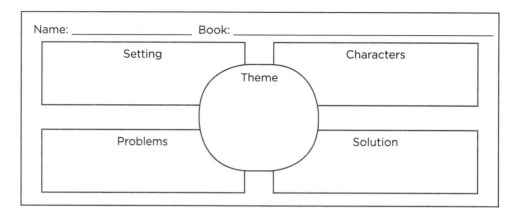

Figure 6.1: Sample story-mapping activity sheet for the primary grades.

*Visit **go.SolutionTree.com/literacy** for a free reproducible version of this figure.*

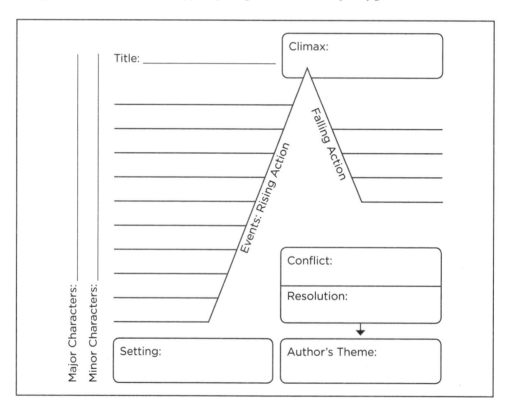

Figure 6.2: Sample story-mapping activity sheet for the secondary grades.

*Visit **go.SolutionTree.com/literacy** for a free reproducible version of this figure.*

★ **Read/respond:** Students use a two-column sheet of notepaper as they read. They record key statements in one column and their responses to them in the other.

★ **Read/retell:** Have your students work with a learning partner. One student reads aloud a portion of the text (only as much as his or her hand can cover). This helps make the task of reading less challenging for the struggling student. The student then retells that portion of the text in his or her own words. The other student reads the next portion (only as much as his or her hand can cover) and restates the big idea.

★ **Reciprocal questioning (reQuest):** For this strategy, students read a passage of informational text silently and stop after each sentence to answer teacher questions. These questions serve as a model of the kinds of questions that students should be asking themselves as they read independently (Gipe, 2005). This process helps students better answer questions after reading and in teacher-facilitated group discussion.

★ **Reciprocal reading:** This strategy begins with the teacher modeling. The students gradually take over, assuming four different roles in the comprehension process.

    i. **Questioning**—Focusing on evaluating their own understanding of the main ideas of a passage

    ii. **Clarifying**—Clarifying confusing portions of text

    iii. **Summarizing**—Determining important information they have learned

    iv. **Predicting**—Determining what they might expect to read next (Palincsar & Brown, 1984)

★ **Rereading:** This does not mean that students reread the entire text. They reread certain parts to answer questions as they go through the chapter or to support opinions they previously stated in their anticipation guide. Rereading can also be used to practice quickly retrieving information by using titles, headings, charts, italicized words, and so on.

★ **RUN:** This strategy is a great reminder for students as they read difficult and challenging texts (Salembier, 1999). Make a poster of the following steps for your bulletin board for all to see.

    ✦ **Read and adjust speed**—Change your speed of reading depending on the level of difficulty of what you are reading.

    ✦ **Use word identification skills**—Look for word clues in sentences or context clues to determine the meaning of unknown words.

    ✦ **Notice and check parts you don't understand**—Put a check mark or sticky note in the margin near text you don't understand so you can go back and reread the section later for greater clarity.

★ **Text tagging:** Develop questions for students before they read a passage of text. Hand out sticky arrow tags for them to use as they read. Model how to use the arrows when they find pertinent information that will assist them in answering the questions. After they have tagged the appropriate sentences, have students synthesize the author's message in their own words.

★ **Think-aloud:** If we expect our students to utilize appropriate comprehension strategies, we need to model them and demonstrate them using think-aloud techniques. In this process, select a short portion of text and give the students a copy of it. Read aloud a portion of the text to students, stopping after each paragraph to verbalize thought processes used to make sense out of the passage. As the students become more confident, encourage them to try this technique when they read with a learning partner.

★ **Topic–detail–main idea:** This strategy helps students identify the overall topic of the passage, supporting details, and the main idea (Jennings et al., 2006). The students read the entire selection first. Then they reread the first paragraph only and state the topic in one or two words. Next, they underline the details that the author shared related to the topic. They proceed in the same manner with the rest of the paragraphs. Then they decide on the main idea of the entire passage based on the topics and details gleaned from each paragraph.

★ **Trio reading:** Students work in groups of three, each taking turns reading portions of the text. This form of round-robin reading is engaging and not as threatening as whole-class round-robin reading, where the struggling student might feel anxiety.

★ **Very important point (VIP):** Give students a large sticky note that has been cut into four to six strips. Model this strategy by reading a text aloud to students, marking the important ideas as you read with a VIP sticky-note strip. Since students will each have a limited amount of sticky-note strips, they need to decide which points are the most important. They share these with a learning partner and are much more prepared for a class discussion at the end of the lesson.

★ **Visual summary:** Encourage students to pause throughout their reading and make a quick sketch of the main ideas they found while reading the text passage. These visual summaries are tools that deepen their understanding of text.

★ **Whisper read alternating paragraphs (WRAP):** Learning partners take turns reading together using this strategy to reinforce text comprehension and boost retention and fluency. Students both listen to the text being read and read the text themselves.

　i.　Place students with a partner. Give them a text selection to read.

　ii.　Direct one student to whisper read the first paragraph while the second student follows along in the text. Partners alternate reading every other paragraph.

   iii. At the end of every page or section of the text (depending on length), have the two students discuss three ideas they learned from the text. Before you begin this activity, ask a student to demonstrate whisper reading in front of the class so students understand how softly they will need to read the text.

★ **Yes/no and why?:** This strategy involves the students answering yes, no, and why questions while they read (Richards & Gipe, 1992). Begin the process by modeling a yes (something the reader liked or understood) and a no (something the reader did not like or did not understand). Then the students do the same as they read and explain their answers (Gipe, 2005).

Strategies After Reading

Activities after reading are particularly important to assist and support struggling readers in organizing and retaining important information from the text. Teachers need to explicitly teach comprehension strategies at each stage of the reading process for students to successfully comprehend informational text.

Considerations for designing lessons to support your students after reading informational texts are:

★ Be sure students know how to summarize and synthesize the main ideas of what they read.

★ Teach students how to reflect on text and make connections that are meaningful to them.

★ Develop students' skill of rereading certain sections of the text for greater clarity.

★ Extend students' learning so that they can see how to apply the information they learned in their lives and clearly see the purpose of the reading.

Techniques to Consider

★ **3-2-1:** This strategy facilitates a quick reflection of the reading or lesson. Ask students to respond in writing to—

   ✦ 3 things they discovered

   ✦ 2 things they found interesting

   ✦ 1 question they still have

★ **Accountability talk:** You can use this strategy during teacher-student conferences, with learning partners, in small groups, or for the whole class. Students discuss the informational text that they just read and make connections while questioning and comparing their own perspectives on the reading, including—

   ✦ Text-to-self connections

   ✦ Text-to-text connections

   ✦ Text-to-world connections (Resnick & Hall, 2001)

★ **Alphabet summary:** Have the students return to the prereading ABC grid chart (see page 69). Now they can complete more boxes based on what they learned from the text, adding one idea or word from the text with one letter of the alphabet (L'Allier & Elish-Piper, 2007).

★ **Cartoon strip:** Students can show what they know and remember from the text by creating a comic strip that depicts the main events and ideas of the passage. Drawing is an excellent way for students to show their understanding of the ideas and a way for them to express themselves creatively. This is a powerful strategy for visual learners.

★ **Cinquain summary:** Have students reflect on what they have read and create a poem to summarize the main ideas. One strategy is to use a cinquain poem that describes a specific subject or idea. It uses the following format.

  + First line—One word/subject
  + Second line—Two words describing line one
  + Third line—Three action verbs that relate to line one
  + Fourth line—Four words, two relating to line one and two relating to line two
  + Fifth line—A synonym for the word in line one

★ **CliffsNotes:** Divide the students into small groups of four to six students. Each team is responsible for writing a chapter summary organized like the popular *CliffsNotes* series.

★ **Collage:** Have students work in small groups to create a collage of words, pictures, and images culled from magazines that capture the main ideas of the text.

★ **Commercial creation:** Students work in pairs to create an advertisement with visuals and written details about concepts they have learned from the reading.

★ **Compare/contrast organizer:** This graphic organizer helps students compare and contrast ideas presented in the text.

★ **Debates:** If the text presents differing points of view, have students prepare their pro and con arguments and stage a debate about the issues as a class. These debates can also be held in smaller teams to maximize involvement.

★ **Discussion:** It is important to engage learners in discussions after reading a text. These can be in a whole group, in a small group, or with learning partners. Students can communicate the ideas from reading with others. In these discussions, students discover their own connections to the text and the meaning of the passage.

★ **Exit card:** Provide short prompts to students to complete after a lesson or after they have completed reading a chapter of the text. They submit these exit cards before they leave the class or after the conclusion of the lesson to provide instant feedback on what they learned and where there are gaps in instruction.

★ **Fishbowl:** Selected students sit in the middle of a circle to discuss the main ideas of the text. Other students can join in the fishbowl as they contribute new information to share. Or divide your students into two groups. Form a circle with chairs and have the first group sit in the chairs. Call that circle the inner fishbowl. After they discuss key ideas from the text, the outer circle can pose questions. Then students switch places.

★ **Found poetry:** Found poetry is a type of poetry created by taking words, phrases, and sometimes whole passages from other sources and reframing them as poetry (a literary equivalent of a collage). Provide students with a variety of magazines. Working with partners, they create a found poem with words and phrases cut out and arranged on construction paper that capture the main ideas of the text.

★ **Guess who/what?:** Students make a list of key terms from a text they have completed. They make a list of characteristics that describe the person, object, or idea from these terms taken from the text. Working with learning partners, they share their written characteristics. This is an excellent tool for review.

★ **Headlines:** Have the students create headlines for the main ideas of the text. Give students a limited number of words that they can use to make their headlines. Put them on sentence strips and display them around the room.

★ **How-to guide:** In this summary strategy, students write directions explaining how to do something related to the subject that they have been reading about.

★ **Just the facts:** Have students work with partners. One student is a newspaper reporter. The other student responds to the important ideas from the text by answering the who, what, where, why, when, and how questions the reporter student poses.

★ **Learning journals:** This strategy involves students writing journal entries about the meaning of what they just read and any personal connections they have made. You respond to each student's journal entry.

★ **Letters:** You can use letters in a variety of ways to review what students have read. Students can assume the role of a historical figure. In addition, you can encourage them to write letters to local businesses, authors, museums, and so on related to the topic they read about.

★ **Magnet summary:** These summaries involve the identification of key terms or concepts from a reading, which students will use to organize important information into a summary. In other words, these are ideas that "stick like a magnet" to boost student comprehension of what they read. Students look for a key term or concept in their reading that is connected to the main idea. This is a magnet word. Students share their magnet words with a learning partner. Then they use these words in a sentence. Lastly, they organize their sentences into a summary of the text or chapter.

★ **One-minute message:** In a one-minute quick write, students write down all they can remember from the reading. They then take turns reading their one-minute message to a learning partner.

★ **One-sentence summary:** Ask students to summarize the passage in just one sentence.

★ **Opinion chart:** Students make a T-chart diagram. On one side, they list the main ideas of the text, and on the other side, they list their reactions to the main ideas.

★ **Paragraph frames:** Write a few structural key words on the board or on the students' papers, such as *first, next, then, now,* and *finally.* The students write what they remember from the text passage in individual sentences under each key word (Gipe, 2005).

★ **Photo captions:** After students read, give them a selection of photographs, postcards, picture cards, and so on that relate to the text they just read. Ask them to choose a graphic and create a caption that captures new information they learned from the text.

★ **Popcorn reading:** Have students select their favorite words, ideas, and phrases from the text. Imagine the class is one large bag of microwave popcorn inserted in the oven to pop. One at a time, in random order, the students "pop" out of their seats and state their favorite word or phrase as an active summarizing technique.

★ **Power notes:** The power notes strategy teaches students an efficient form of organizing information from an assigned text. This technique provides students with a systematic way to look for relationships within the material they are reading. Power notes help visually display the differences between main ideas and supportive information in outline form. Main ideas or categories get a power 1 rating. Details and examples get power 2s, 3s, or 4s. This systematic approach is helpful for struggling readers because it visually displays information and its importance (Santa, Havens, & Valdes, 2004).

★ **Quotes and notes:** Fold a sheet of paper in half. At the top of one column, write "Quotes," and on the other column, write "Notes." Have the students write the most important quotes from the text on one side and their reactions and responses on the other side. They then share these with a learning partner.

- ★ **RAFT:** RAFT is a writing strategy that helps students understand their—
  - ✦ **R**oles as writers
  - ✦ **A**udience they will address
  - ✦ **F**ormats for writing
  - ✦ **T**opics they'll be writing about

  This more extended writing activity expands on topics covered in the informational text. RAFT assignments encourage students to uncover their own voices and formats for presenting their ideas about content information they are studying. Students learn to respond to writing prompts that require them to think about various perspectives.
  - ✦ Who are you as the writer?
  - ✦ To whom are you writing?
  - ✦ In what format are you writing?
  - ✦ What are you writing about? (Santa et al., 2004)

- ★ **Retelling pyramid:** After students read a chapter of a nonfiction text and are familiar with the concepts of main idea, details, author's purpose, text structures, and so on, have them complete a retelling pyramid. This strategy is best done in pairs. The pyramid should contain the following concepts (Ellery & Rosenboom, 2011).
  - ✦ One word describing the major idea (the top of the pyramid)
  - ✦ Two words describing a detail
  - ✦ Three words describing another main idea
  - ✦ Four words describing another supporting detail
  - ✦ Five words describing the author's purpose
  - ✦ Six important vocabulary words
  - ✦ Seven words describing reader's aids
  - ✦ Eight words telling what you have learned (the bottom of the pyramid)

- ★ **Rhyme, rhythm, rap:** Students work with a learning partner to discuss the key concepts and supportive details of the text. They jot these ideas down and create a rhyme, rap, or rhythmic phrase to help them remember. This not only boosts their comprehension and retention but also is a creative way to foster students' musical talents.

- ★ **Role play:** Ask students to take on various roles depicted in the text. This is a particularly powerful strategy for reenacting historical texts.

- ★ **Roundtable review:** Give students a chance to create a roundtable review of the informational text by talking about what intrigues them, interests them, confuses them, and so on about the text.

- ★ **Save the last word for me!:** This technique allows students to summarize what they have read, connect what they have read to their world, share implications and applications, make inferences, and draw conclusions with each other. This discussion strategy requires all students to participate as active speakers and listeners. Its clearly defined structure helps shy students share their ideas and ensures that frequent speakers practice being quiet. It encourages meaningful classroom conversations by eliciting differing opinions and interpretations of text.

All students in the group create a quote card from the reading. The first student reads one of his or her quotes to the group and shows where to locate it in the text. The student isn't allowed to make any comments about his or her quote until the other members of the group give their reactions. Then the student gets the last word in the discussion of the quote. This process continues until everyone in the group has shared at least one quote and has provided the last word in the discussion.

★ **Semantic feature analysis:** This strategy uses a grid to help students explore how concepts relate to one another. By completing and analyzing the grid, students see connections, make predictions, and master important concepts. They not only examine related concepts but also make distinctions between them according to categories and criteria. This strategy enhances comprehension and vocabulary skills. Figure 6.3 shows an example of this grid.

	Has Fur	Has Feathers	Can Fly	Can Be a Pet	Runs on Four Legs	Lays Eggs
Dog	X			X	X	
Cat	X			X	X	
Rabbit	X			X	X	
Lion	X				X	
Duck		X	X	X		X
Pony	X			X	X	

Figure 6.3: Sample semantic-feature analysis grid.

*Visit **go.SolutionTree.com/literacy** for a free reproducible version of this figure.*

★ **Semantic mapping:** This strategy has the students graphically representing and connecting the main ideas they just read in the text using a graphic organizer (see page 55). This tool helps struggling readers who may be spatially challenged see and connect information in ways other than a linear outline. The start of the map should be from memory, and then students can return to the text to extend and embellish the map with more details.

★ **Sequence chart:** This type of graphic organizer helps students recognize organizational patterns in text, steps in a process, points on a timeline, and the importance of sequential order. After selecting a text that would benefit from such support, give students this graphic organizer. Students can write a brief label or key phrase for each step or event. This presents a visual timeline of the main ideas for the student. See figure 6.4 for an example of a sequence chart.

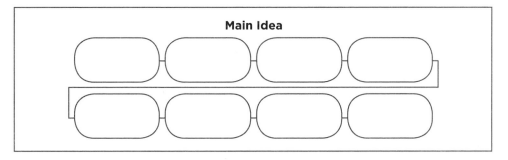

Figure 6.4: Sample sequence chart.

*Visit **go.SolutionTree.com/literacy** for a free reproducible version of this figure.*

★ **Shape poem:** Shape poems are a great way to summarize key ideas from any subject area. Students select an object that relates to the main idea of the informational text they have read. They brainstorm words related to that subject and then use those words to make the shape of the object in a word design pattern.

★ **Slogan:** Have students review their notes or consider the main ideas covered in the text, and ask them to create a slogan that summarizes the main idea of the text. Have the students write their slogans on sentence strips and post them around the room to serve as visual memory links to reinforce learning.

★ **Snowball:** Distribute blank sheets of white paper to the students. Have them write down three of the most important ideas they learned from the text. Ask students to then crumple the paper up into a round ball (resembling a snowball). Everyone stands, with his or her snowball in hand. At the count of three, they gently toss their snowballs in the air and catch somebody else's snowball. Then they take it back to their seats, open it, and find out what was important to another student. This is a favorite energizer and effective summarizer best done at the end of the class period or right before recess, since it does tend to excite the students. Struggling students feel successful with this activity because their responses are anonymous.

  Other prompts for this activity include—

  ✦ Write down three new vocabulary words from the text.

+ Write down three new ideas you learned.
+ Write down three questions for homework. (The person who catches the snowball answers the questions.)

★ **Synectics:** This strategy fosters creativity, divergent thinking, and comparisons (Gordon, 1961). Students can use it to take a fresh look at something they know and connect it to new knowledge in the form of an analogy. When comparing two objects or ideas, show a picture of one common object, and have students compare it to the topic they just read about. You could also do a verbal synectics activity and ask students to compare the topic you are studying to—
+ Something you would find in a toy store
+ Something you would find in the refrigerator
+ Something you would find at a hardware store
+ Something on the beach

The metaphors and analogies can be catalysts to writing or doing a symbolic summary. See figure 6.5 for a sample synectics activity.

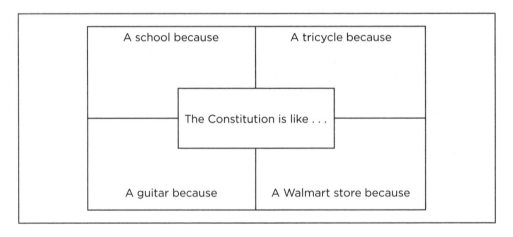

Figure 6.5: Sample synectics chart.

*Visit **go.SolutionTree.com/literacy** for a free reproducible version of this figure.*

★ **Take five:** Students answer the question, What five words would you use to describe _____? Students then create a poster for the word wall.

★ **Test maker / test taker:** Having students write their own review tests for a text passage and share them with a learning partner is a powerful learning tool. This helps students decide on the main ideas and the most relevant information. In addition, it connects them back to the text for closer reading as they compose and answer questions.

★ **Think links:** This summarizer strategy involves asking students to write the text topic in the center of a piece of paper. Then ask them to surround what they have written with details or links that relate to the topic (Wilson, 1981).

★ **Top-ten lists:** This is a fun and creative way for students to summarize the main ideas of the text. The first step is for students to list facts about the subject matter. Interesting or unusual items become the basis for their lists. If coming up with ten items is a bit challenging, students can make a "fab five" list.

★ **Twitter post:** Using just 140 characters, students create a tweet that summarizes main ideas from the text.

★ **Umbrella:** The structure and design of this graphic organizer helps students see how the main ideas relate to the supporting ideas of a lesson or text. Using the metaphor of an umbrella, students visualize that the main idea covers the details (the raindrops). Students fill in the main idea on the umbrella and the supporting details in the raindrops.

★ **Wanted poster:** After reading the text, students can create a wanted poster about the subject they are studying. These posters can include pictures and facts that capture the main ideas of the reading. Displaying these posters in the classroom provides a creative review and an excellent visual memory of the ideas from the text.

★ **Whip-around:** This verbal summary strategy involves total participation and data gathering. Display open-ended prompts and ask students to verbally complete the phrases after reading the selection. This is a positive strategy for struggling readers because it provides them with other insights and ideas and models of text-based thinking. Some prompts to consider are—

  + I learned . . .
  + I discovered . . .
  + I was surprised . . .
  + I am beginning to wonder . . .
  + I now realize . . .
  + I want to find out more about . . .

Final Thoughts

Develop your own toolbox of techniques to support struggling readers in comprehending informational text. Some of the best practices include:

★ Teaching self-monitoring strategies

★ Modeling for and teaching students how to use the think-aloud strategy

★ Beginning by telling students what you want them to know and the outcomes of the lesson

★ Using techniques to activate and build background knowledge about the topic

★ Preteaching difficult academic vocabulary words and their meaning so that students will have greater access to the meaning of the text

★ Teaching organizational skills

★ Providing ample time for students to practice these comprehension strategies with a learning partner and then independently

After all, the ultimate goal for teachers is to instill in your students the skills and strategies that will assist them in their lives beyond the classroom. By utilizing the strategies presented in this chapter and integrating them into the fabric of your curriculum, you can help your students become more skilled in comprehension so they can achieve independent success with informational text in school and in their future beyond school.

7   Questioning Techniques to Foster Higher-Level Thinking

Increasing reading comprehension through questioning techniques is a vital instructional strategy. Struggling readers tend not to ask themselves questions as they read. Questioning helps students engage with text and make sense of what they read. The ability to generate questions while reading not only increases attention and alertness but also strengthens comprehension (Farstrup & Samuels, 2002). Other benefits of questioning include:

* ★ Sharing ideas and connections about the text or lesson
* ★ Involving students in the lesson
* ★ Identifying and exploring different types of information
* ★ Increasing interest and engagement
* ★ Fostering creative thinking
* ★ Supporting independent learning
* ★ Reviewing previous learning and lessons taught
* ★ Evaluating students' knowledge
* ★ Monitoring completion of work or reading
* ★ Assessing achievement of lesson outcomes, goals, or standards
* ★ Stimulating extension of learning with peers
* ★ Having students self-assess and modifying or extending their thinking
* ★ Encouraging wonder, rather than just reciting answers
* ★ Using mistakes as opportunities to learn
* ★ Synthesizing and evaluating what was learned
* ★ Making connections between content and real-world application

Since teachers spend a considerable amount of their instructional time asking questions, the focus of this chapter will be on making the questioning process more effective to raise student achievement. How can you ask your students better questions, and how can you help them become more involved in the questioning process to increase their engagement? Questioning needs to become part of the fabric of every classroom. Teachers need to model how to ask questions while reading and guide students about how to dig deeper into the text with questioning.

Types of Questions

Lesson planning is all about lesson *mastery*, not lesson *mystery*! Teachers must develop questions that focus on how that mastery will take place. What do I want my students to learn? How am I going to get them there? How will I know that they learned it? The content and goals of your lesson will determine the kinds of questions you will ask students to engage their thinking. For example, in developing a meaningful discussion of a book or a story, you need to identify important information presented in the text to promote creative questioning, not just factual recall.

Let's look at some basic types of questions.

Closed Questions

Closed questions have short-response answers that can be found in the text. They often start with words such as *list, name, who, what, where, when,* and so on. Researchers often consider closed questions as a lower-level recall of facts. They are appropriate to:

★ Do a quick check of factual details
★ Look for specific strengths or weaknesses
★ Review content
★ Synthesize information and details

In Bloom's taxonomy (Bloom, Engelhart, Furst, Hill, & Krathwohl, 1956), a hierarchy of increasingly complex intellectual and thinking skills, closed questions are at the knowledge level or comprehension level and are most appropriate and successful with students at the primary level to boost recall.

Some closed-question prompts you can try include the following.

★ Where would you look in the book (or story) to find the answer?
★ Where does it state that? Show me.
★ What clues helped you in finding this answer?

Yes/No Questions

These are closed questions with a single response. They significantly reduce the opportunity for discussion. Sometimes teachers might have to use yes/no questions for the sake of time; however, do not use yes/no questions exclusively. If they are used, follow up with more probing prompts, such as, "Why did you think that? How do you know?"

Open Questions

Elicit more in-depth responses from students with open questions. The story or text does not always obviously state the answers to these questions. Rather, the reader needs to infer or draw his or her own conclusions. This level of questioning is more challenging for the struggling reader. Open-ended questions often begin with prompts such as *what if, why, how, explain, discuss, decide,* and so on. Examples might include:

* Do you think _____?
* How is _____ different from _____?
* What background knowledge do you have about this topic?
* What would happen if _____?
* What predictions are you making?
* How could you look at this information differently?
* What questions do you have as you read?
* Can you describe _____?
* What are you wondering about the book, topic, or _____?
* What is your opinion of _____?

These higher-level questions are more appropriate for:

* Encouraging group or partner discussions
* Allowing students to find out on their own
* Inviting students to think more creatively
* Interpreting content
* Encouraging more critical thought
* Fostering deeper thought
* Making connections with text and the real world

The questions need to vary depending on the age and ability levels of students and the content or topic you will be discussing. In addition to asking questions at various levels of Bloom's taxonomy (knowledge, comprehension, application, analysis, synthesis, and evaluation), try to alternate between open and closed questions as well.

Considerations in Planning the Right Questions

When planning questions to use with students, you must first decide on the objective of the lesson and the goal for asking the questions. This will help you decide on the type of questions to ask. Remember to focus on the important information that you want students to remember from the lesson—not on trivial facts that would be the focus of "gotcha" questions.

* Think about follow-up prompts for yes/no questions so students get beyond just focusing on recalling the facts.

★ Scaffold your questions so that you start with more literal, informational questions, moving up in a sequenced way to more challenging questions that require critical thinking.

★ Prepare your questions ahead of time so that they build on one another and are congruent with your objectives.

★ Make sure your questions are specific and utilize vocabulary that students know and recognize.

★ Avoid ambiguity when creating questions and misconceptions that might confuse your students.

★ Make sure that you don't include the answer as part of the question. In other words, don't give away too much information.

★ Be clear about the response that you expect from students. Do you want them to explain, define, draw a symbolic summary, retell, or expand?

★ Consider how you will ensure student participation. Will a response be required?

★ Consider what you will do if a student provides an incorrect response.

★ Decide on how many questions you should ask and when.

★ Ask a colleague to observe a sample lesson, paying particular attention to the types of questions you ask.

An important part of questioning, particularly for struggling readers, is the concept of wait time. *Wait time* is providing students with adequate time for processing the question and considering their responses. Research supports that pausing for wait time will increase academic achievement (Casteel & Stahl, 1973; Rowe, 1986; Stahl, 1990; Tobin, 1987). There are two phases of wait time. The first is the length of time a teacher waits after asking a question before calling on a student to respond. The second phase is providing time for the student to process. For lower-level, closed questions, allow at least three seconds for the student to respond. This increases to at least five to eight seconds for more complex, open-ended questions. To help your students feel more comfortable and confident in responding to questions, you can pause after asking a question and allow the students to practice their responses first with a learning partner before class discussion begins.

In classrooms, the average wait time when questioning is not sufficient for students, especially those who are struggling with processing. Mary Budd Rowe (1986) discovered that when a period of think time lasts at least three seconds, many positive things happen to students' and teachers' behaviors and attitudes. Some of the benefits include an increase in the length and correctness of student responses and a decrease in the number of "I don't know" responses. The amount of wait time depends on the age of the student, the content of the material, the depth of analysis you are asking for, and the student's confidence level.

Rowe (1986) finds that increasing wait time relates to positive student outcomes, including improved achievement and comprehension, more in-depth responses, more developed student interactions, and more engagement. Another study by Kenneth Tobin and Bill Capie (1982) examines the effect of wait time on student engagement. Tobin and Capie looked at features such as responding to a question, attending to an assignment, and explaining information. They conclude that using higher-level, open questions and increased wait time contributes to enhanced student engagement and time on task.

Teachers must focus on asking the right questions to develop the higher-level thinking skills critical for the focus on 21st century skills and the Common Core State Standards. As a teacher, learning to ask better and deeper questions comes with time and experience. How do we help our students think creatively and critically at any age?

In her blog post, "5 Powerful Questions Teachers Can Ask Students," Rebecca Alber (2013) identifies five simple open-ended questions that she has found elicit the greatest results from her students. These questions would be suitable for any topic and for most grade and ability levels.

1. **What do you think?** This question allows the student to respond based on his or her own background knowledge. By asking this invitational question, you are not revealing too much.
2. **Why do you think that?** This takes the student to the next level of thinking because he or she has to provide a reason for his or her response.
3. **How do you know this?** This invites the learner to reflect on and connect to the reading to substantiate his or her statements. The student can also make connections to his or her own life and experiences that he or she can then connect with the ideas or text.
4. **Can you tell me more?** The student is encouraged to expand and extend his or her response and go deeper with the information.
5. **What questions do you still have?** This puts the responsibility on the student to think critically and to reflect on what he or she is wondering and wants to find out more about. This is important because it leads to further study and investigation.

Student-Generated Questions

Students already ask teachers many questions. However, these questions tend to be more procedural or for clarification on an assignment. Our goal as teachers should be to foster the skill of generating thoughtful and critical questions that reflect a level of analysis, self-monitoring, and active knowledge seeking. Students need to ask questions to connect to and make meaning out of what they are reading and learning.

Questioning helps students learn and explore at a deeper level. Unfortunately, the emphasis in many classrooms is on the answers that students give instead of on fostering a sense of inquiry.

Encouraging students to become more "question friendly" by shifting to a culture of more student-generated questions will foster this sense of inquiry. Struggling readers need additional support in this process because they tend not to ask questions as they read. So teachers should model how to ask questions as they read. This will increase student motivation and interest in the reading. It also helps students set a purpose for reading as they make personal connections with the text.

The activities that follow will help students before, during, and after reading and will increase comprehension. To activate prior knowledge and to speculate, students should ask questions before they read. Self-questioning during reading helps students engage more fully during the reading process. Asking questions after reading stimulates further connection making and provides extended learning opportunities. Effective teachers demonstrate how to turn the information they are learning into questions. The value of questioning as an active reading strategy should not be underestimated (Marzano et al., 2001).

Providing students with strategies to create and ask questions that extend their learning can help them clarify any confusion they might have and encourage them to share their wonderings so you can guide them (Tovani, 2011). Asking questions gives students more self-reliance, confidence, and control over their reading. Teachers need to be very purposeful in creating a culture of inquiry in the classroom, especially since students might perceive asking questions as a weakness.

You can also use student questions as an informal assessment tool. Being aware of student questions will inform your practice and provide a launchpad for your lesson planning, and you can then modify the content to meet individual student needs. Students' questions can help you differentiate instruction based on their understandings. Have your students jot down their questions as they read, either on sticky notes in the margin or on think-pad sheets that they turn in to you.

Before you implement the questioning strategies explored on the following pages, be sure to model how to create different kinds of questions, sometimes referred to as "thick" and "thin" questions. *Thin questions* are literal, factual-response questions, whereas *thick questions* invite the reader to go deeper and really think about his or her response. Provide practice with both types. For example, one way to do this is to brainstorm with them a list of questions that they might ask after reading. List them on the board. Then show them how they can extend these knowledge-based questions into more creative responses by adding a phrase that fosters more critical-thinking skills. The questions they generate at first require factual, knowledge-based responses. However, if you rephrase those questions into more open-ended responses, their thinking goes deeper and the responses are much more divergent.

★ What would you do if _____?
★ How might this look different if _____?
★ What are some other ideas about _____?
★ Can you imagine _____?
★ What if you _____?
★ What do you think will happen next?
★ What are the reasons?
★ What was the process?
★ What is your reaction to _____?
★ What are the benefits of _____?
★ Why do you think this happened?

Techniques to Consider

Teaching students how to ask questions inspires reading with purpose and different ways of thinking. Ask yourself how you can promote more meaningful questioning and student inquiry in your classroom. When the classroom is a safe atmosphere for exploration with many opportunities to discover, questions naturally emerge. Try the following questioning strategies.

★ **Question-card relay:** To introduce this strategy to your students, explain the characteristics of a relay race. You might mention teamwork, speed, and passing something along. Write these themes on the board before moving on to the question-card relay.

   After you deliver a lesson, or the students have read a story or a chapter in a text, distribute an envelope to each student with three blank index cards inside. Ask the students to think of a question—something they are wondering about related to the text—and write it on the outside of the envelope, putting their names in the corner. Have the students form groups of four to six. When you give a signal to start, each student passes his or her envelope to the student to the right. They all read the question they have been given, remove a blank card from the envelope, and write their responses on the card. If they are unsure of the answer, they respond to the best of their ability. Set a specific time for response—usually one to two minutes, to keep the activity quick and engaging. Then signal for students to pass the envelope on. Students sign their responses and tuck them into the envelopes, passing the envelopes on to the next student. This time, they get a new envelope with a new question on the outside. They write their responses and sign their names on another blank card in the envelope. The process continues until all three cards contain responses. When you give the final signal, the envelopes go back to their original owners.

After the students review their peer responses, collect the envelopes and use the responses as a formative assessment tool. Students get answers to their questions and examine others' questions from the text, and you get information about students' insight into the text. You can also use questions from the activity on tests or quizzes.

For struggling students or English learners, this activity is best done in pairs so that students can share their questions and answers with each other.

★ **Postcard to my teacher:** After students have developed the skill of asking questions as they read, have them jot down a question on a card for you. Then all students place their cards in a large mailing envelope addressed to you, putting your classroom number on the outside of the envelope. The last student to deposit his or her question in the envelope seals and "mails" the envelope to you.

This exercise allows students to practice writing questions, responding to the text on their own as they ponder the possibilities of "turning the tables" on their teacher. You are also able to use this as a formative assessment tool by noting the level of complexity and the different levels of thinking that students have used in developing their questions.

★ **5 by 5:** In this strategy, you ask students to come up with five questions about a topic in a five-minute period. They do not need to answer the questions—just create them. Depending on the age and ability level of the students, this activity could be expanded to 10 by 10, with ten questions generated in ten minutes. This process of writing questions helps them practice and brainstorm so that they are more responsive to what they are reading and will probe more deeply into the information.

★ **Five whys:** Challenge students to come up with five why questions for the reading or lesson. Since most students have developed a habit of asking why, this strategy allows them to build on this skill. Let them think creatively and use this exercise in inquiry to foster their curiosity. They work with a learning partner, taking turns asking each other their why questions. A modification is to use a why–what if–how sequence of questioning to extend the questioning.

★ **Wonder journals:** Begin your class with a question of the day from the wonder journals that students write in daily—notes that they take when they are wondering about a story, text, topic, lesson, or picture.

★ **Wonderful wonder walls:** Have students create "wonder walls" with illustrations from their wonder journals (posted like graffiti on a wall) related to what they are curious about. Questions written on sentence strips can be part of these displays. Classmates can respond to the questions on blank paper posted on the wonder walls. This helps create an environment of inquiry.

★ **Curiosity corner:** Dedicate a portion of your classroom as a "curiosity corner." This space can serve as a treasure trove of artifacts that students may be curious about. Place an assortment of objects in the corner that they can hold, touch, and feel to investigate more deeply, such as artifacts that support a unit in science. Encourage questioning and critical thinking as they explore these objects.

★ **Wonder walkabout:** With their wonder journals in hand, students walk the neighborhood around your school. This is a particularly powerful exercise for primary students, making them aware of the world around them while they use all their senses. They record what they experience on the walk, share their thoughts, and form questions based on their observations.

Question Cube

The question cube is a motivating tool to differentiate curriculum using choice and chance. It allows students to respond with six variations of a task to complete related to the content of the lesson. Further differentiation can occur if teachers color-code the cubes to correspond to various readiness levels, student interest, or student learning styles.

To use it as a questioning strategy, duplicate a cubing pattern on cardstock or construction paper (see figure 7.1, page 100). Write a different task, question, or prompt on each side of the cube so the cube can be used for multiple lessons. Students cut out and build their own cubes using tape or a glue stick. Younger students can make a cube out of a child-size milk carton (with the top cut and folded flat). One question is placed on each side of the carton. Some basic prompts for the cubes include:

★ Who?

★ What?

★ Where?

★ Why?

★ When?

★ How?

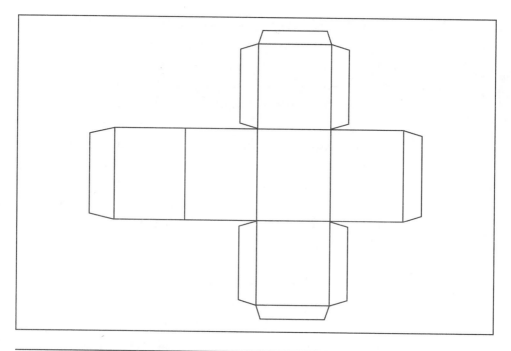

Figure 7.1: Question cube pattern.

*Visit **go.SolutionTree.com/literacy** for a free reproducible version of this figure.*

The procedure for implementing the strategy includes three main steps.

1. Students read a story with a learning partner and pause to roll the cube.
2. They answer whatever question appears on top based on the facts of the story or the text they have read.
3. Then another student rolls and responds to the question.

You can prepare an accompanying worksheet in advance to give the students more detail about the expected outcomes. You can also use dice as an alternate to the cube, where each number corresponds to a question listed on a worksheet.

Following are question prompts that fit into the various levels of Bloom's taxonomy of higher-level thinking skills.

Remembering

★ How do you explain _____?
★ When did _____ happen?
★ Can you list the _____?
★ What is _____?
★ How did _____ do it?
★ How was it that _____?
★ Where is _____?
★ Who was _____?

★ What were the main _____?
★ How would you explain _____?
★ Can you name the _____?
★ Why did _____?
★ Can you list three _____?
★ Can you find the meaning of _____?
★ What do you recall about _____?

Understanding

★ What ideas demonstrate _____?
★ How would you restate _____?
★ What is the theme of _____?
★ How would you define _____?
★ Can you tell me more about _____?
★ What facts support this idea?
★ How would you generalize _____?
★ What is meant by _____?
★ What strategies might you use to distinguish between _____ and _____?
★ What differences are there between _____ and _____?
★ Why is _____ happening?
★ What do you think could have happened next?
★ What could be a reason for _____?
★ Will you restate _____?
★ Who do you think _____?

Applying

★ What would happen if _____?
★ Could this have happened in _____?
★ How would you support this idea from the text or lesson?
★ What would be your solution for _____?
★ How would you relate _____ to _____?
★ How might you group characteristics such as _____?
★ How would you sequence _____?
★ Why is _____ important?
★ Can you clarify why _____?
★ How is _____ an example of _____?
★ What questions would you ask of _____?

Analyzing

- ★ What is the overall main idea of _____?
- ★ What conclusions can you make about _____?
- ★ How is _____ related to _____?
- ★ Why do you think _____ happened?
- ★ What events could have happened?
- ★ What conclusions can you make about _____?
- ★ How would you differentiate between _____ and _____?
- ★ What evidence do you have about _____?
- ★ How would you categorize _____?
- ★ How might you compare _____ with _____?
- ★ What are the advantages and disadvantages of _____?
- ★ What are some of the problems with _____?
- ★ What evidence in the text can you find that _____?
- ★ How would you justify _____?
- ★ What reasons can you give for _____?

Evaluating

- ★ How would you verify _____?
- ★ Is there a better solution to _____?
- ★ Can you develop a hypothesis for _____?
- ★ Judge the value of _____.
- ★ How would you explain _____?
- ★ How would you evaluate _____?
- ★ What information from the text could you cite that would support _____?
- ★ How would you modify _____ to develop a different _____?
- ★ What would happen if _____ were true?
- ★ How could you change the outcome of _____? Why _____?
- ★ Do you think _____ is a good or bad thing and why?
- ★ What would you have done if _____?
- ★ How would you prove or disprove _____?
- ★ What could be done to reduce _____?
- ★ What could be done to increase _____?
- ★ How effective are _____?

Creating

- ★ Can you develop a possible solution to _____?
- ★ In what ways would you prioritize _____?
- ★ Tell me how to justify _____.

★ Why did you choose _____?

★ Can you design a _____ to _____?

★ What are the implications of _____?

★ How would you test _____?

★ How would you rationalize the outcome of _____?

★ In what ways is it better to _____ than _____?

★ How could you change or modify _____?

★ Do you agree with the outcome of _____? Why?

★ What decision would you make about _____?

The question cube think pad (figure 7.2) is designed to accompany the cube to more carefully describe directions and tasks in open-ended ways. You can customize the think pad to fit your subject area, your content area, or the level of difficulty based on the age and ability level of your students.

Topic	
Describe It What do you see as the main points of the lesson?	**Compare It** What would you compare this topic to? What are the similarities? What are the differences?
Associate It What does this topic relate to?	**Analyze It** How would you break this subject into component parts?
Apply It What are some ways that you can use these ideas?	**Argue for or Against It** Take a stand on this topic; argue for or against it.
In the space below, write a paragraph about the topic based on your cubing answers. Add your team's responses as well.	

Figure 7.2: Question cube think pad.

*Visit **go.SolutionTree.com/literacy** for a free reproducible version of this figure.*

Final Thoughts

The strategic use of questions in the classroom can truly deepen learning, foster a growth mindset, and allow students to transform their thinking practices. A great question invites exploration and wonder and fosters higher-level thinking skills. A teacher who has mastered the art of questioning can create learning situations for success for all students while covering the content material deeply and fostering a greater sense of comprehension. You can improve your questioning skills using the techniques described in this chapter.

The next chapter explores the idea of developing an action plan for literacy success with a focus on organization, management, and planning.

8 Developing an Action Plan for Success

This final chapter provides a blueprint for success in your literacy program. So far, this book has examined the characteristics of struggling readers, instructional practices, student engagement strategies, and intervention tools. Now we will explore how to organize and manage your literacy classroom, design an action plan, receive ongoing professional development, and maintain and accelerate literacy achievement for all your students.

Reaching your struggling readers requires dedication, commitment, and an integrated literacy program across the content areas and grade levels. As struggling students move up through the grades, the curriculum and knowledge continue to build and the achievement gap widens unless intervention steps are taken. If students aren't proficient readers, they will fall further behind. Literacy skills are the key to student success.

It is important to provide new information for struggling readers in multiple contexts over time (Allington, 2012). In today's classrooms, nothing is more essential to successful teaching and learning than strategy-based instructional techniques that engage even the most reluctant and struggling student. Repeated but meaningful practice can significantly increase students' potential for success. This can be a daunting task and challenging for busy teachers like you who are trying to accomplish too much in too little time. Give yourself permission to take baby steps on your journey to reach and teach all your students. Try one strategy at a time. You need to feel successful as well. The strategies in this book are designed to empower you, the classroom teacher, to implement an effective course of action that makes a difference for student achievement.

To access multiple pathways of student learning, be flexible and allow time for practice and reinforcement. Successful repeated practice has to be more than rote repetition; rather, practice should tap into multiple modalities for your students. Give students opportunities to listen, observe, visualize, move, interact, investigate, record, discuss, revisit, and so on. This propels learning forward as students interact with text and the information they learn in more meaningful ways.

According to R. David Pearson and Linda Fielding (1983), a successful literacy program designed to increase comprehension has four elements.

1. Large amounts of time dedicated to actual reading of text
2. Explicit, teacher-directed instruction in comprehension strategies
3. Opportunities for peer and collaborative learning
4. Adequate time for multiple responses to reading, including time to talk with the teacher and one another about the reading

The goal is for students to learn information in numerous contexts throughout the curriculum through different methods of delivery. Students have many opportunities to apply what they are learning, and you will be able to reinforce that learning.

Acceleration Versus Remediation

What are some ways to instill in our struggling readers that can-do spirit? Richard Allington (2012) and others believe in the power of acceleration versus remediation. In practice, this means focusing on what your students are ABLE to do instead of focusing on their deficits (Southall, 2007).

A—Assess

★ Begin instruction at the student's entry point to learning.
★ Provide ongoing and formative monitoring of student performance.
★ Determine what needs to be adapted or modified.

B—Build

Build skills in core learning areas to form building blocks to literacy success.

★ Increase phonological awareness.
★ Master phonics (including the alphabetic principle and word identification).
★ Increase fluency (reading rate and automaticity).
★ Develop vocabulary (word knowledge and retrieval, and word meaning and concepts).

L—Link

Link learning strategies to skills for transfer.

★ Present instructional components frequently over time.
★ Integrate the skills so that students see themselves as readers.

E—Engage

Engage students with interactive and collaborative formats.

★ Students need an opportunity to respond frequently and in different ways.

Maximize your instructional time with struggling readers (and all readers) to make every moment count. "Sit-and-get" instruction does not work. Focus more on engagement and flexible grouping patterns in the classroom. For struggling readers, small-group, one-on-one, and collaborative activities truly make a difference in meeting students' individual needs in a supportive context. While stretching the students from where they are to where they need to be, provide varying levels of support, and select learning experiences that increase transfer of learning and maximize growth potential. It is important to engage struggling readers in learning experiences that foster growth through rich discussions and that promote higher levels of thinking to reinforce or extend learning.

Instructional Accommodations to Consider

Teachers are often asked to modify instruction to accommodate the special needs of their struggling students. In fact, all students will benefit from the practical and easy-to-implement strategies in this book. Let's take the mystery out of adapting materials and strategies for struggling readers and instead focus on creating a supportive learning environment that celebrates the strengths of all students. Here are some ingredients to consider in your inclusive classroom.

- ★ Group size
- ★ Frequency of instruction
- ★ Chunking of information
- ★ Consistency of message
- ★ Collaborative learning opportunities
- ★ Making connections
- ★ Engagement strategies
- ★ Checking for understanding
- ★ Reflection
- ★ Support structures
- ★ Variety of exposures
- ★ Multiple contexts
- ★ Repetition and reinforcement
- ★ Time on task
- ★ Choice
- ★ Formative and ongoing assessment

Flexible Grouping for Maximum Success

Planning an instructional program for struggling readers requires careful attention to the delivery of instruction and the setting. This involves looking at a variety of grouping strategies. The days of fixed-ability groups are over. To create a positive literacy learning environment, you must consider other factors, including time, resources, space, student need, and content. Grouping depends on the purpose, content, setting, and needs of the students.

Flexible grouping allows students to be part of many different groups so the student needs can be met based on their readiness, interest, or learning styles. Groups can be student selected, teacher selected, purposeful, or random. Choose the best criteria to support the desired learning outcomes (Tomlinson, 2001).

Whole-Class Instruction

Direct and explicit instruction is critical so that all students hear the same message. Instruction needs to be carefully planned and organized for the greatest impact. Even though instruction is given to a whole group, you still need to be aware of meeting individual needs. Student engagement is also critical. Integrate interactive segments into the whole-class lesson to ensure retention.

Small-Group Instruction

Small groups need to be flexible and are excellent settings for more targeted instruction for students who need extra support. The size of the group should vary by need and the content being discussed. Groups should not be static and should change in size and membership throughout the year.

Learning Partners

Having students work in pairs provides an excellent opportunity to reinforce and extend concepts that you have taught. Student-to-student interaction can be a great motivator. Clearly define procedures and outcomes for the best success.

Side-by-Side Instruction

This is the most powerful form of instructional support; however, the realities of time constraints and class size often limit the time you can allocate for such support. Side-by-side teaching may include valuable time listening to the student read, conferencing with students, discussing strategies for comprehension, or previewing texts a student will read.

Keys to Direct Instruction and Interactive Teaching

In this model of interactive teaching, Anita Archer promotes gradual scaffolding of instruction, leading to giving students more success at independent work (Archer & Hughes, 2011).

I Do It

★ Model and provide clear rationale.
★ Use examples and nonexamples to demonstrate.
★ Use think-aloud strategies.
★ Assist students to notice certain aspects of instruction.

We Do It

★ Encourage choral response for shorter responses.

★ Use partner response for longer responses.

★ Use structured pair-share.

★ Don't forget repetition as needed.

★ Practice!

You Do It

★ Students respond individually (orally, in writing, or with gestures).

★ Students do homework to practice.

★ Students answer questions in class.

★ Students keep thinking and remain focused by responding in other ways.

How to Promote More for Struggling Readers

Certain classroom practices, procedures, and routines provide an inclusive and supportive atmosphere in the classroom. It is important to pay attention to how the classroom is organized as well as to your instruction delivery. Table 8.1 has some helpful hints. The right column is a good reminder of how you can help struggling readers succeed in your classroom.

Table 8.1: How to Help Struggling Readers Succeed in the Classroom

The More Struggling Readers Get . . .	The More Struggling Readers Need . . .
Ability grouping	Flexible grouping
Frustration-level texts	Supportive scaffolds
Lecture	Increased time on task
Pencil-and-paper tasks	Peer collaboration
Phonics in isolation	Authentic applications
Low-level thinking	Critical thinking
Skill and drill	Reinforcement over time
Low-quality instruction	High-quality instruction
Gotcha questions	Strategic knowledge
Diminished expectations	Positive reinforcement
Outside interruptions	Multiple applications

Best Practices for Looking at Literacy in Your Classroom

All teachers need to strive for comprehensive, balanced literacy programs, including small-group instruction. Think about the students in your classroom. How many of them are successful at reading and can understand most of the text? How many of them can read with ease and understand even the most challenging text? How many of them cannot read or understand the text? How can a packaged program with the same instruction meet all their needs? It definitely can't. Differentiation is the key.

So what are the best practices for students who are struggling? This book has explored more than two hundred strategies to support student success in reading. Consider the following key ideas as you determine which strategies, tools, and techniques you will choose for your students.

★ Spend more time on reading and writing to develop students' skills (Allington, 2012). How can they get better without adequate practice?

★ For high accuracy and good comprehension, most reading should be "easy" reading at students' independent reading level for greater fluency. Do all your students have copies of texts at the appropriate complexity level? Do students have an opportunity to choose their own books?

★ Comprehension strategies should not simply ask students to answer literal questions at the end of the chapter after reading. Active comprehension strategies (as described in this book) need to be explicitly modeled and taught every day. This also holds true for content-area subjects.

★ Students do not develop decoding strategies from skill-and-drill tactics. You must actively teach decoding strategies on a daily basis with spelling and writing.

★ Students benefit from an integrated and comprehensive literacy plan and curriculum guide. Do students learn from reading? Are standards shared with the students?

★ Some students need more intense instructional support and enhanced opportunities to read and write with scaffolded instructional support. Do struggling students need an opportunity to read and write more daily? Yes!

★ Critical-thinking skills are now linked to literacy learning. Basic literacy competence will not suffice anymore. Literacy skills need to be expanded to include summarizing, organizing, synthesizing, comparing, analyzing, creating, and evaluating texts—necessary 21st century skills.

★ Developing independent readers and writers is critical to developing thoughtful, lifelong learners. We need to focus on personal ownership of literacy and independent reading and writing activities.

★ Good classroom instruction is critical to a student's success.

Final Thoughts

No single model, packaged program, reading series, best curriculum, or magic bullet will succeed with every student in every classroom. No quick fix will make a true difference. An effective literacy program requires time, resources, collaboration, and a commitment to a clear vision. Don't waste your time seeking out the best packaged program. Instead, focus on student success. Teachers, you make the difference!

Teacher's Toolbox

Students deserve the best strategies educators can offer to ignite their interest and excite them about reading. I gathered this toolbox of easy-to-implement techniques from classrooms throughout the United States during my years of teaching as a general educator, special educator, and literacy coach. I now have the privilege of teaching teachers, and I see these strategies used with great success in their classrooms.

30-Second Speech

After students have read a chapter or story or learned new information in a lesson, provide them with think time to make sense of the content.

- ★ Pose a question to the class.
- ★ Ask students to prepare a thirty-second speech about the main ideas they learned and their answer to the question.
- ★ Students then deliver their thirty-second speech with a learning partner.

This process enhances literacy skills and fosters social interaction.

ABC Summary

Use this strategy to activate the beginning of a lesson or as a tool for summarizing at the end of a lesson. Give students an ABC grid (see page 69) with an empty box for each letter. They can work independently, in pairs, or as a team to complete their grid with words starting with that letter that relate to the topic they are studying.

A-B Each Teach

This shared reading strategy helps students process information as they take turns reading to each other in pairs. Ask each partner to read a section of the text silently. Then students teach their portion of text to their partner in their own words. The process continues as each partner reads and retells a portion of the text. This strategy is ideal for struggling readers because it helps curb anxiety related to reading aloud to an entire class.

Advertising

Choose an idea or concept from a lesson you are teaching or from the text or story students are reading. Have the students make a newspaper or magazine advertisement for the concept. Post the ads around the room.

Agreement Circles

Students form a circle. Read a statement related to the reading or lesson. If a student agrees with the statement, he or she takes a step inside the circle and discusses his or her opinion with the students in the outer circle.

Best Test

Ask students to work in small groups to create their own "best test" from what they have learned in the lesson, text, or story. This empowers students and encourages higher-level questioning skills as they generate tests that they then give their learning partners.

Billboard

Students work in teams to create billboard ads for their favorite books. Post the billboards around the room to inspire curiosity and wonder about students' favorite titles.

Board Game

This is a more time-intensive activity. Ask students to work in small groups to create a board game that features the key ideas of the informational text or the story they have just read.

Book Trailer

Students are familiar with movie trailers and previews of coming attractions. This activity asks students to work in small groups to create a video advertisement to pique the interest of new readers. To do this, students need to understand the message of the book, the main ideas, the characters, and the plot. Students also practice their persuasive writing skills as they create a script for their video.

Brainstorming

Pose a question or share a topic of discussion with the whole class or a small group related to the reading students have done. Ask students to share their ideas and responses. They can write down their answers on chart paper. Use a ball toss (students share their ideas when they catch a ball tossed around the room) to add a kinesthetic element to the strategy.

Carousel Cruising

This strategy encourages teamwork and provides opportunities for reading, writing, speaking, and listening.

* ★ Place chart paper on the walls around the room.
* ★ On each piece of paper, write different but related topics or questions as prompts.
* ★ Divide the class up into small groups, and ask each group to stand next to a piece of chart paper.
* ★ Tell each team to choose a recorder. The recorder should use a different colored marker to record his or her team's responses on the chart.
* ★ Instruct students to move around to each poster when you give a signal. They should review ideas recorded on the chart and then add their own in a different color.
* ★ When teams have answered all the questions, have groups do a gallery walk to review the posters. Or, alternatively, a team reporter can share three main ideas from the team's original poster, including the additional contributions of others.
* ★ As a variation, students can record their ideas on individual sticky notes and then place the ideas on the appropriate chart.

Character Grid

Create a grid with the names of main characters from a reading listed vertically down one side and a list of their qualities or characteristics horizontally across the top. Ask students to work in teams to complete the grid, putting a check mark in the corresponding trait column. Students should then discuss their grids with their team members.

Choral Reading

Ask students to read a poem, a paragraph, or a passage from a story or text out loud and all together. This helps build fluency for struggling readers as they hear the cadence of the words flow together in this oral language activity. Students can read aloud one or two lines individually as their confidence with the passage increases.

Circle Around

Have students form two equal circles, one inside the other, with students in the inner circle facing the students in the outer circle. Students should then ask each other questions about a review topic, either student or teacher generated, depending on the students' age and ability level. After the first question-and-answer exchange, direct students to rotate ("Take five steps to the right," or "Move to the left three students"). A variation is for one circle to ask questions about a reading while the other circle responds, or students share their journal entries with their circle partners.

Cloze Call

Use this strategy to help students use new vocabulary words in context. Modify a text or passage that the students have been reading. For example:

★ Leave the first sentence of a passage intact and then add additional sentences with every seventh to tenth word omitted and replaced with a blank space.

★ Ask students to guess an appropriate word that relates to the overall meaning of the passage.

A variation is to provide students with a choice of three words for each blank or passage.

Collage Creations

Have students work in small groups to create a collage of words, pictures, and images that capture the main ideas of a story or chapter of a text they have read.

Commercial

Choose an idea or concept from a lesson you are teaching or from the text students are reading. Have students write a television or radio commercial for the concept and present their commercials to reinforce their learning and boost their speaking and listening skills.

Concept Map

Students can use this brainstorming strategy independently or in pairs or small groups. Place a word or topic in the center of a piece of paper or a poster. Have students add qualities, characteristics, ideas, images, and feelings that relate to the word or topic in the center of the concept map.

Concentration

This activity reinforces vocabulary words and their definitions.

★ Create vocabulary word cards and corresponding definition cards, one word or definition per card.

★ Ask students to work with partners, placing all the cards facedown on the desk.

★ They then take turns flipping over cards and trying to match words with their corresponding definitions, removing the pairs when a correct match is made.

★ Provide an answer sheet for students to check their work.

Comic Strips

Comic strips are the perfect tool to teach students sequencing and that there is a beginning, a middle, and an end to a story.

★ Choose several comic strips from the newspaper, cut out the individual panels, and mix them up.

★ Ask students to find their "comic strip buddies" who have frames from the same comic strip.

★ Challenge students to put the comic strip panels in order from beginning to end.

★ For an extension activity, have students change the dialogue in the speech bubbles and then sequence them.

Comic Strip Compare/Contrast

Choose two comic strips and ask students to use a Venn diagram to compare and contrast them. Do this first as a partner activity after you have modeled it. Then give students two new comic strips to compare and contrast on their own. This helps students learn the skill of compare and contrast and requires deeper-level thinking.

Consultation Lineup

This strategy fosters a sense of collaboration and inclusion. Students boost their speaking and listening skills as they discuss topics.

★ Decide on a topic to discuss.

★ Ask students to sit in two rows facing a partner.

★ Partner A shares his or her idea or question about the topic with partner B.

★ Partner B brainstorms responses and adds to the idea.

★ Partner A records new ideas or answers.

★ Partner A moves one student to the left (like musical chairs) so that new partners are formed.

★ The roles are then reversed, and partner B shares an idea or question and partner A responds while partner B records.

★ Repeat the process and reverse roles with new partners several times.

★ Students then review their notes and create an action plan and summary paper.

Create a Comic Strip

Once students have some experience with sequencing a comic strip and changing the dialogue, challenge them to create their own comic strips.

★ Provide students with a blank sheet of paper that has three frames on it.

★ Encourage students to come up with a comic strip that summarizes the key events in the story or text that they have read.

★ Then have students add details such as a background, props, and at least two characters with dialogue bubbles.

Dear Author

After reading a book, students write a letter to the author about how they felt about the story, which can then be mailed to the author. This is a great way for students to practice their skills in writing a letter, but with a real purpose. They can comment on whether they liked or disliked the ending, if they think an alternative ending would have been better, and if they would like to see a sequel to the book. They can ask the author questions, such as, How did you get the idea for this book? How long did it take you to write this book? and What was your favorite book as a child?

Declare It With Dots

This is a preassessment tool to check students' background knowledge regarding a topic.

★ Select a topic that students will be studying or reading about.

★ Create a poster with four quadrants: (1) new concept, (2) somewhat familiar, (3) beginning understanding, and (4) comfortable with the concept. Place it on the wall.

★ As students enter the classroom, give each one a colored dot, and ask them to place it in the appropriate quadrant on the poster that reflects their understanding of the topic.

This is a helpful tool to get a snapshot of the students' background knowledge to inform lesson planning for the unit of study.

Directed Reading Thinking Activity (DRTA)

This comprehension strategy guides students in asking questions about a text, making predictions, and then reading to confirm or refute their predictions. Students are encouraged to be active and reflective readers.

★ Activate students' thinking prior to reading a passage by asking them to scan the title, chapter headings, illustrations, and other text features.

★ Students read a portion of the text until you ask them to pause, reflect, and connect. This process continues until the text is complete.

★ Students then make connections with the text and discover if their previous predictions are confirmed or not. It is important that they find supporting statements in the text. Then continue the discussion, asking them:

  ✦ What do you think about your predictions now?

  ✦ What did you find in the text to prove your predictions?

  ✦ What did you read in the text that made you change your predictions?

Dramatic Monologue

Have students create a monologue for a character in a scene of a book or story they have read. Ask them, "What is the character really thinking at that moment?" Act it out.

Every Pupil Response (EPR)

Distribute index cards, small paper plates, or individual whiteboards to students. When asking a question, tell students, "This is an EPR alert!" All students should answer with yes/no cards, or they write their answer on a plate, card, or whiteboard and hold it up. With this activity, you can tell at a glance who understands or gets the correct answer.

Fact or False?

Ask students to write two true statements about what they read and one false statement. They then quiz each other to determine if their partner can recognize the false statement. This is a great way to get your students to dig deeper into the text in order to be specific about their questions and also to challenge their partner's responses.

Fist of Five

With this hands-on assessment strategy, you can check for understanding mid-lesson or at the end of a unit or chapter. Ask students to raise their "fist of five" in the air if they understand the concept and main ideas of the lesson. They show four fingers if they feel fairly confident in their understanding, three fingers if they are okay with it, two fingers if they do not understand, and one finger if they need help.

Flash Facts

Provide the students with three index cards. Pause during a presentation, during a lesson, or while they are reading a text or story, and have students create a flash card with one of the main ideas or a key concept or vocabulary word. At the end of the lesson or reading, students work in pairs and review their flash card facts as a quiz with their learning partner.

Foggiest Point

Ask students to pause during their reading or reflect after their reading and jot down their "foggiest point" so far. What do they need clarification on? What don't they understand?

Foldables

This is a hands-on technique where students can create their own foldable book or graphic organizer to help them remember key concepts from the text or lesson. There are multiple types of foldables available to use in the classroom. Students cut and fold to construct these tools, which can be used to study strategies and quiz each other, as vocabulary sheets, visual maps, and much more. An Internet search yields many samples of foldables.

Gallery Walk

Gallery walks are a great way to get students out of their seats and moving around the classroom. It is important to stress the procedures and routines for this exercise. Divide students into small groups (corresponding to the number of posters or stations around the room). They then rotate through the stations within the classroom. Each station may consist of a question or a brief activity to complete. Give a signal for students to rotate to the next poster or station. Students might have clipboards to respond to stations as they rotate around the room. Students can also make their own contributions by adding their ideas to what is already listed on chart paper.

Generating Interactions Between Schemata and Text (GIST)

GIST is a summarizer strategy students can use both during reading and after reading (Richardson & Morgan, 2000). Students create summaries that are twenty words or less (for narrative or informational text) that help them gain a better overall understanding of the material they just read. First, model this technique on the board. Then students work with learning partners. After completing their summaries, the teams share their GISTs and try to synthesize them to create a group GIST summary. This exercise works best with shorter passages (see figure A.1).

Get the GIST

Name: _____   Title: _____

Source: _____

1. Read the article or section of text.

2. Fill in the five Ws and Hs.

Who: What:

When: Where:

Why: How:

3. Write a twenty-word GIST summary.

_____   _____   _____   _____

_____   _____   _____   _____

_____   _____   _____   _____

_____   _____   _____   _____

_____   _____   _____   _____

Figure A.1: GIST summarizer strategy tool.

Visit go.SolutionTree.com/literacy for a free reproducible version of this figure.

Graffiti Board

For this brainstorming activity, students use sticky notes to record their responses. Pose a question or a topic on a blank sheet of chart paper. Give students think time to write their responses to the question or concept on a sticky note. They first share with a learning partner and then place their individual sticky notes on the chart paper—the graffiti board. This is a powerful strategy for struggling readers and English learners because they do not have to write too much and they can even draw a picture as their response. The important thing is that everyone participates. You can use this activity as an assessment tool as you visualize students' knowledge of a topic or to check for understanding. Students can then group and categorize their responses to develop their critical-thinking skills.

Guess Who?

Prepare a list of important people your students have been learning about, including main characters from stories, history texts, and so on. Print these on construction paper and tape them to the back of each student (without letting him or her see the card). Students try to guess who their person or character in a story is by asking questions that only require yes or no answers.

As a variation, conduct the same activity using vocabulary words. The students ask yes or no questions in an effort to guess their word.

Headlines

Students come up with a headline that captures the main message of the reading, a text, or the lesson. These headlines can be written on sentence strips and mounted on the classroom walls.

Human Bingo

This is a variation of a cooperative learning structure (Kagan, 1989). In this human scavenger hunt, students interview other students using a bingo card with questions from the lesson or text they are studying. At the signal, students interview each other to see if they know the answer to one of the questions on the bingo card. When a student knows the answer, that student signs the bingo sheet and moves on to another student to interview.

Idea Wave

This is a summarizer strategy best utilized at the end of a lesson or after completing a reading. Students do a quick write of three to five ideas they remember. Start an "idea wave" at one spot in the room with one student. Then the next student responds rapidly, and then the next, one after the other until a wave of ideas continues throughout the room, ending with the teacher's response.

Jumbled Scrambled Summary

After students read a text passage or story, present randomly ordered words and phrases from the material. The students work in pairs to unscramble the words and phrases in a logical order to reveal the main ideas.

Last (First) Word Acrostic

This strategy can either be an activator to tap into students' background knowledge about a topic or a summarizer to help check for understanding. Give students the topic. They write the topic, one letter at a time, vertically along the left-hand side of a piece of paper. Give students a short amount of time to come up with one word related to the topic that starts with each letter. Students can share these acrostic poems and then post them around the room.

Learned-Affirmed-Challenged (LAC)

LAC is a strategy for engaging in debriefing and reflecting on written content. It encourages students to (1) identify new learning from what they have read, (2) affirm what they already knew, and then (3) identify questions they have or how the new learning may challenge their thinking.

The three goals for LAC can be posted on the board. Once students complete their reflection individually, they can share with a learning partner or with a group of four students. Finally, the whole class will discuss what was learned, affirmed, or challenged.

Learning Lineup

Learning lineups can serve as an activator or a summarizer.

★ Using it as an activator, students complete an anticipation guide reflecting on their opinions and beliefs about a topic they will be studying or reading about. Using it as a summarizer, students jot down their responses to review questions first.

★ Students form two parallel lines facing each other.

★ Students get time (usually sixty seconds) to share their responses to a given question or statement with the partner facing them.

★ Give students a signal (a bell, a chime, and so on). One line, the "movers," shift as one student moves to the end of the line and the rest shift to face a new partner. The students in the other line are the "shakers." They shake in place while the movers shift.

★ Provide a new prompt and continue the activity.

List, Group, Label

This strategy is a brainstorming process that helps students organize their understanding of specific vocabulary and concepts. This technique builds on students' prior knowledge and reinforces their categorizing and labeling skills.

★ Select a main concept in a reading selection.

★ Have students brainstorm all the words they think relate to the topic (list). Visually display student responses.

★ Divide the class into small groups (group). Each group works to cluster its list of words into categories.

★ Invite students to suggest a heading or label for the groups of words they have formed (label).

See figure A.2.

Name: _____

List, Group, and Label

Directions: Brainstorm some words that are related to your topic. Then sort those words into different categories. Label each category.

Topic: _____

Brainstorm	Label: _____	Label: _____	Label: _____

Figure A.2: List, group, and label brainstorming tool.

*Visit **go.SolutionTree.com/literacy** for a free reproducible version of this figure.*

Literacy Cafe: Reading Response Menu

This is an engaging process that allows students to make choices and teachers to differentiate instruction. After you have taught a lesson or the students have completed a chapter of text or a story, create a reading response menu students can choose from. Figure A.3 (page 122) is an example of a format and sample tasks.

Most Important Word

This strategy can work for both fiction and nonfiction reading. Students select what they think of as the most important word of the book. They then illustrate it and can even create a Wordtoon (see http://wordtoons.com).

Directions: Choose an appetizer, a main course, and a dessert from the menu.

Appetizer
- What predictions can you make about the text?
- Why did you choose this book?
- What do you picture in your mind as you visualize this text or story?
- What do you already know about this topic?

Main Course
- Write a summary of the chapter you read. Include character, setting, and main events.
- Was there something special about the author's writing that you liked? Describe it.
- Why is this a good story? Give five good reasons.
- What character do you think was most important? Why?
- What text features did you notice in this book? List four to six and explain how they helped convey information.

Dessert
- Summarize the text in four or five sentences.
- How did the main character change from the beginning of the story until the end?
- List one major cause-and-effect relationship that occurred in the story.
- When you finish the story, write an idea to relate a prequel (events that happened before the story took place).
- What questions do you still have about the topic?
- Draw a picture and write a paragraph about your favorite part of the story or chapter.

Figure A.3: Literacy cafe menu.

Most Valuable Point (MVP)

Ask your students as they read to keep in mind, "What is the most valuable point?" Students review their notes and decide on the MVP of the text and record it along with the reasons why they think that the idea is the most valuable. Students share their MVP with their learning partners.

Movie Review

In this activity, students play the role of movie critic for a newspaper and write a critical account of the book as a journalist. They share their reviews with others in the class.

Mystery Word

Ask a student to volunteer to sit in the front of the room so that his or her back is to the class word wall. Ask one student to select a "mystery word" from the word wall. The student in the seat asks questions about the key vocabulary word until he or she guesses it. This activity can also be played with weekly vocabulary words. Clues can include:

★ The definition
★ A synonym
★ A rhyming word
★ An antonym
★ The ending letter
★ The beginning letter

One-Minute Paper

Ask students, "What was the most important thing you learned?" and "What questions do you still have?" Set a timer for one to two minutes for this quick-write activity. Then have students work with learning partners to share their ideas. This activity also works during class time as a brain break.

Open Mind Diagram

This strategy has students break up into small groups of four. Within the groups, each student will get a different colored marker. The students form the shape of a head on a piece of paper and write inside the head. The information they write inside the head comes from the story or text, including quotes or questions they may have.

This strategy is beneficial for the struggling reader because he or she learns from the information others share. This is an excellent way for students to prepare for a test or project, or to organize information (see figure A.4 for a sample open mind activity).

Some prompts to share with students could include "Write two phrases," "Draw two symbols," "Record two quotations," or "Share your own ideas, reflections, and connections."

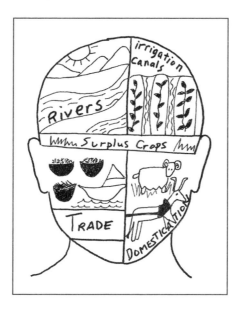

Figure A.4: Open mind activity.

*Visit **go.SolutionTree.com/literacy** for a free reproducible version of this figure.*

Pair, Compare, and Share

In this activity, learning partners work on skill and practice questions. One student answers the first question while getting coached by his or her partner to make sure the answer is correct. Then the roles are reversed. The next stage is for the pairs to share with another pair of students and coach as a team. If all agree on the answers, the process continues. However, if they disagree, they do independent problem solving, dig deeper to make connections with text, and then ask for clarification as needed.

Pantomime Parts

Divide a story or informational text that students are reading into sections. Students form small groups. Each group is responsible for a certain section of the text. One member of the team is the narrator, and the rest act out the text using pantomime as the narrator, reads the section of text.

Picture This!

This is an excellent review strategy for new vocabulary words. Have students fold a blank sheet of paper into eight sections. In each section of their paper, students make a quick sketch or a graphic symbol that represents one of the key vocabulary words of the week or from the text.

Popcorn Reading

Provide a brief passage for students to read. Have them jot down words or phrases that are particularly meaningful to them. When you give the signal, students pretend they are kernels of popcorn popping. They pop up in random order and shout out their important word or phrase for the rest of the class. This activity provides a great review of the main ideas, and students learn from each other to boost comprehension and retention.

Post-a-Problem

This strategy gets students involved in group discussion and can be used in many different content areas. The purpose of this process is to facilitate group discussion, creative thinking, and problem solving. Also, this technique encourages revision of questions as alternate answers are found.

★ Students form teams. Provide each group with a topic to discuss related to the lesson or the text.

★ The small group then generates a review question and an appropriate answer that the team agrees on.

★ The question is written on one side of a note card with a *Q* on it, and the answer is on the back of the card with an *A* on it.

★ The questions are then passed to another group.

* When the group of students receives a question card from another team, they read it and write the answer to the question individually.
* Team members then compare and discuss their answers.
* If they agree and reach consensus, they turn the card over to reveal the answer from the team that sent it.
* If they do not agree with the sender's answer, they write their own answer down as an alternate response.
* They receive a new question card, and a second student reads that question, and the process continues until all teams have had a chance to answer all questions.
* Lead a class discussion on what students learned from this process.

Postcard Pen Pals

Distribute postcards and ask students to write to a friend (or a character) about their feelings about a book or story.

PQRST Study Strategy

This process is helpful to increase comprehension and retention of informational text.

* **Preview:** Students preview the text by skimming over the title, pictures, headings, and so on.
* **Question:** Students look at the questions at the end of the chapter and ask their own questions to help focus their reading.
* **Read:** Students read the text to answer the questions generated and to take notes of the main ideas.
* **Summarize:** Students work with a learning partner taking turns summarizing the main ideas of the text.
* **Test:** Students test their generalizations with the supporting information in the text. If they can't support their generalization, they need to dig deeper with text connections.

Priming the Pump

Engaging students in projects that involve deeper critical thinking in response to reading extends learning. Some examples include:

* Writing and illustrating a story about a problem
* Creating a poster or a mural depicting a particular period in history or a topic in mathematics or science
* Writing a script and performing it
* Making a product from the lesson and then developing a marketing plan for it
* Producing a class newspaper or a parent newsletter about a topic or idea from the text
* Creating a picture or word collage of the main ideas of the text

P.S.

After students read a story or book, have them create a new ending. They can work with a learning partner as they create an epilogue that describes what could happen to the characters next.

Question-Answer Relationship (QAR)

The question-answer relationship (QAR) strategy helps students understand the different types of questions and strategies for answering them. There are four types of questions (Raphael & Au, 2005).

1. **"Right there"** questions can be answered directly from the text. The answers are found in the reading. Often the words used in the question are the same words found in the text.

2. **"Think and search"** questions require the reader to read more deeply between the lines. The answers are not so obvious and require analysis based on the information in the text.

3. "**Author and you**" questions are based on information provided in the text, but the student is required to relate it to their own experience. Although the answer does not lie directly in the text, the student must have read it in order to answer the question.

4. **"On my own"** questions require the student to recognize that he or she must first consider the question before developing an answer. The answer comes from his or her own experience and background knowledge, which is used to make connections with the ideas in the text.

Have students work together to form questions about the text, find answers, and share with the whole class. Ask students to write down questions and answers.

Question Fans

For this exercise, you create color-coded question fans that students can use with each other after they read a story. It is a fun way of encouraging students to ask and answer questions and provides support for sequencing questions. The questions on the fan should be open-ended enough to be suitable for any story. Duplicate the questions on colored cardstock, cut into strips, and hole-punched at one end where a paper brad can be inserted to hold the pieces together and create a fan shape. Model the process first before students work with learning partners.

Some sample questions include:

★ Can you name the _____?
★ What are the main differences between _____ and _____?
★ What do you think will happen next, and why?
★ If you read between the lines, what is suggested about _____?

★ How has _____ changed by the end?

★ Why is the structure important to _____?

Reading Response Charts

Have students draw a T on their papers. On one side, they write three interesting quotes from the text or story. On the other side of the T, they respond with a personal connection or paraphrase what the quote means to them.

Roving Reporter

This is an excellent way to keep tabs on small-group activities and an opportunity to synthesize the multiple issues being discussed about a topic. Designate one of the students from each group as a "roving reporter." These students move from group to group with a clipboard to record notes and ideas that they can glean from other groups to share with their home group. It is interesting to have a discussion of the similarities and differences the reporters find.

See-Think-Wonder

This visible-thinking tool is used to guide students' questions and observations. It boosts their critical- and creative-thinking skills as well.

★ Present a visible image or an artifact for the students to look at and examine.

★ Give students a piece of paper with three columns labeled *see*, *think*, and *wonder*.

★ After the students have had a chance to examine the picture or object, they jot down what they see, what it makes them think about, and what they are wondering.

This activity is a catalyst for conversation and creates a need-to-know opportunity for the upcoming lesson or reading.

Sentence Frames

This strategy provides an opportunity for structured oral language development. Because of the scaffolding used to practice speaking and writing in complete sentences, it is beneficial for struggling readers and English learners as well. The process also provides an opportunity for structured academic talk and support for language acquisition.

★ Ask students a question related to the story, chapter, or lesson.

★ Provide a sentence frame on how the student will answer the question. Simple sentence frames require students to provide basic information about the sequence of events in a story, for example, "The problem in the story is . . ."; "This is a problem because . . ."; "The problem is solved when . . ."; and "In the end . . ."

★ Record student ideas on the board or on a chart for all to see.

★ Students read orally their responses to the sentence frame.

★ Display the sentence strips in the classroom.

Shades of Meaning

This strategy helps students discover how shades of meaning can really make a difference in their speaking and written language vocabulary. The purpose of this exercise is to generate multiple synonyms for key vocabulary words.

★ Go to your local paint store or hardware store and get paint sample strips (the kind that have six to eight different shades of the same color with slight variations).

★ At the base of the strip, write a key vocabulary word.

★ Have students form teams, with each team selecting a paint strip.

★ For each of the different paint color squares, the students work in pairs or small groups to write a synonym for the vocabulary word.

★ Then students trade paint strips.

★ Ask students to create a brief paragraph using several of the synonyms (shades of meaning words) from the various strips to practice using these words in context.

Shoe Partners

This is an example of a random grouping strategy. This fun, interactive brain break allows students to mix and mingle in new and different ways to share with learning partners in the class. Each student looks around the room and finds someone who is wearing shoes that are similar to his or her own shoes. Students can do this by matching color, style, brand, and so on. Once they find their shoe partner, students get a question or prompt to discuss.

Snowball Summary

This is an energizing summarizing activity. Distribute blank white sheets of paper to students. Have them write down *1*, *2*, and *3* (big and bold) on their papers. Ask them to reflect on the lesson or reading. Have them jot down three new ideas they learned today in class. Give them think time and time to write. After they have completed listing the three ideas, have them crumple their paper up into a ball that looks like a snowball. They are to stand, snowball in hand. Tell them to keep in mind two words, *randomly* and *gently*. Instruct them to gently toss their snowball into the air randomly and catch somebody else's snowball at the count of three.

After the students catch a snowball, they take it back to their seat, open it up, and read what was important to somebody else. Some variations include:

★ Write down three new words you learned today.
★ Write down three successes you had in my class today.
★ Write down three things you remember from today's reading.
★ Write down three questions for homework from our lesson or text today. (Whoever catches the snowball has to answer the questions for homework.)

Students get very excited with this activity. Therefore, it's best to do it during the last three to five minutes of the class period, right before recess, or right before students go home.

Take Five

Give each table group five words from the reading, the lesson, the word wall, or the spelling list, and give each group five minutes to create a skit, song, poem, dance, poster, or pantomime using the selected words. Depending on the age and ability level of the students, as well as the time allotted, you may want to adjust the number of words used, or the time allocated.

Talking Trios

Students form triads and share ideas verbally on a topic selected from the lesson or reading. One student starts the response, and each of the triad, in turn, shares in order. This is done as a round-robin exercise without interruption, comments, or questions. This process ensures that everyone has a turn before it becomes a class discussion or triad discussion.

Timeline

This is a particularly powerful strategy for a historical novel. Have the students work with a learning partner and create a timeline of events from the book and corresponding historical events at the time. This can be done on butcher paper and posted on the classroom wall. In developing the timeline, it is helpful to use sticky notes so that it remains flexible until agreement is reached about the accuracy of the information displayed.

Traffic Lights

Create a set of cards for each student to signal you if he or she understands or needs help. If students have a green card displayed, that is a signal that means "I'm good to go" and "I've got it!" If they have a yellow card showing on their desk, it is a caution signal that means "I'm not sure." A red card is a stoplight signal for the teacher and means "Stop!" "I don't get it," or "I'm lost."

Triangle-Square-Circle

This strategy helps students focus their thinking as they reflect on a lesson or a text they have read. As they summarize their thoughts, it helps them make sense out of the information. Give students a simple graphic organizer, or they can create their own.

★ After a lesson, have students draw a triangle and next to it write down three important points from the lesson or reading.

★ Next, have students draw a square and write down anything that "squares" with their thinking or anything they agree with. Students use the space next to the square to record their thinking: what matches their own thoughts, beliefs, or emotions.

★ Finally, have the students draw a circle and next to it write down anything that is still "circling" in their head or questions that they have after the lesson or reading.

Once completed, the graphic organizer can be used for a classroom discussion to synthesize and apply the new information. A variation for primary grades is to use it as a whole group with the teacher charting student ideas. This activity can be used as a closing activity, as an exit ticket, or as a formative assessment of students' understanding of a lesson.

Up and About

This is a reflection activity and a brain break that combines writing with movement to increase comprehension and retention.

★ Select the concept or main idea that you want your students to explore. Some possible topics include:
  + What was the most interesting part of our unit (or story)?
  + What part of the text confused you?
  + What are the most important ideas you remember?

★ Give students three to five minutes to write down what they know (as an activator) or what they remember (as a summarizer).

★ After writing down their ideas, students stand, mix, and mingle as you play some upbeat music.

★ When the music stops, students find someone near them share their ideas with.

★ When the music resumes, they continue to mix and share with others.

Visualization

This is an excellent brain break—having students pause in their reading or in the lesson and visualize the key ideas. Tell the students to "turn on the TV in their minds." After they visualize, have students create a quick sketch of what they were picturing in their minds.

Vote With Your Feet

This strategy can be used as an activator or a summarizer. Because it involves students expressing their opinions about a topic, idea, or question, it is also an excellent formative assessment tool.

★ Have students respond to a list of questions or statements, indicating if they agree, strongly agree, disagree, or strongly disagree.

★ Place signs for each of these responses in different corners of the room: A, SA, D, or SD. If a student is uncertain, he or she stands in the middle of the room.

★ As each statement is read, students "vote with their feet," going to the corner that represents their opinion.

★ In their corner, they pair up with another student and discuss their reasons for selecting that response.

★ Read the next question or statement. Students once again move to the appropriate corner and find a learning partner to share with.

★ Follow the activity with a group discussion.

Voting

As an activator activity, post three statements on the board for students to ponder regarding the upcoming unit of study or the topic of the text they are to read. For younger students, these statements can be made verbally. Students consider which statement is the most important idea in their opinion. They share their response with a learning partner. Then read each statement one at a time and pause for students to raise their hands if they voted for that one as the most important. Affirm each response, and encourage students to look around and see who voted like them. This is an inclusive activity designed to create a need to know about the upcoming lesson. It is not about getting the right answer because all responses are validated. Students feel safe sharing their opinions.

Word Cone

This strategy helps students develop a more vivid vocabulary for speaking and writing. They draw an ice cream cone on their paper. On the cone, each student puts a "dead word." This is an overused, trite, boring word to use in writing and speech. Some examples include *nice*, *said*, and *big*. Students then place "scoops" of rich, more colorful and vibrant words on top of the cone by drawing ice cream scoops on top of the cone. Inside each scoop is a sensational synonym to embellish the boring word. The dead words are then buried in the dead word cemetery. Students are not allowed to use these words in their writing or speaking. For example, if the dead word is *said*, some of the scoops could be *exclaimed*, *shouted*, *bellowed*, and *declared*.

Word Tree

With this vocabulary strategy, provide a root word to students. They "plant" the root word underground in a template of a tree with many branches. Tell the students to work with learning partners and see how many words they can think of that have that root word in it. They place these words on the many branches of the tree. This becomes their personal word bank for that root word.

Wows and Wonders

At the end of a lesson or when students have finished a chapter of the text or read a story, they complete their Wows and Wonders sheet. Have them list at least three to five wows—what they think is important that they learned—and at least one or two wonders—things they are wondering about, such as questions they have and what they don't understand.

Writing Round-Up Relay

This strategy works well with open-ended questions that can have multiple responses.

* ★ Have students work in small groups of four to six.
* ★ Each student should have one sheet of lined paper and a pencil.
* ★ Each student puts his or her name on the paper and numbers the lined spaces.
* ★ Pose a question with multiple answers or a statement that could be expanded with many details. For example, give students a question about a topic from the current unit of study.
* ★ Give a signal for each student to write one idea or answer on line one.
* ★ Then students pass their papers to the student to their right when you give another signal.
* ★ Students respond on line two of the new paper.
* ★ The process continues swiftly in this quick-write relay.
* ★ Students need to read previous responses before they write down their answers so there will not be any repetition of answers.
* ★ When all have had a chance to write their responses, students get their original papers back with multiple responses to the original prompt. This is an excellent way for students to reflect on what they remembered from the lesson or reading in a fast-paced way.

References and Resources

Alber, R. (2013, October 31). *5 powerful questions teachers can ask students* [Blog post]. Accessed at www.edutopia.org/blog/five-powerful-questions-teachers-ask-students-rebecca-alber on January 18, 2016.

Allen, J. (1999). *Words, words, words: Teaching vocabulary in grades 4–12*. Portland, ME: Stenhouse.

Allington, R. L. (2012). *What really matters for struggling readers: Designing research-based programs* (3rd ed.). New York: Pearson.

Alvermann, D. E., & Boothby, P. R. (1986). Children's transfer of graphic organizer instruction. *Reading Psychology, 7*(2), 87–100.

Anderson, C. (2005). *Assessing writers*. Portsmouth, NH: Heinemann.

Anderson, J. (2005). *Mechanically inclined: Building grammar, usage, and style into writer's workshop*. Portland, ME: Stenhouse.

Anderson, R. C., & Nagy, W. E. (1992). The vocabulary conundrum. *American Educator, 16*(4), 14–18, 44–47.

Angelillo, J. (2005). *Writing to the prompt: When students don't have a choice*. Portsmouth, NH: Heinemann.

Anglin, J. M., Miller, G. A., & Wakefield, P. C. (1993). Vocabulary development: A morphological analysis. *Monographs of the Society for Research in Child Development, 58*(10), i–186.

Archer, A. L., & Hughes, C. A. (2011). *Explicit instruction: Effective and efficient teaching*. New York: Guilford Press.

Atwell, N. (1998). *In the middle: New understandings about writing, reading, and learning* (2nd ed.). Portsmouth, NH: Boynton/Cook.

Ausubel, D. P. (1963). *The psychology of meaningful verbal learning*. New York: Grune & Stratton.

Baumann, J. F., Kame'enui, E. J., & Ash, G. E. (2003). Research on vocabulary instruction: Voltaire redux. In J. Flood, D. Lapp, J. R. Squire, & J. M. Jensen (Eds.), *Handbook of research on teaching the English language arts* (2nd ed., pp. 752–785). Mahwah, NJ: Erlbaum.

Baxendell, B. W. (2003). Consistent, coherent, creative: The 3 C's of graphic organizers. *Teaching Exceptional Children, 35*(3), 46–53.

Bear, D. R. (2000). *Words their way: Word study for phonics, vocabulary, and spelling instruction.* Upper Saddle River, NJ: Merrill/Prentice Hall.

Beck, I. L., & McKeown, M. G. (1983). Learning words well: A program to enhance vocabulary and comprehension. *The Reading Teacher, 36*(7), 622–625.

Beck, I. L., McKeown, M. G., & Kucan, L. (2002). *Bringing words to life: Robust vocabulary instruction.* New York: Guilford Press.

Berger, W. (2014). *A more beautiful question: The power of inquiry to spark breakthrough ideas.* New York: Bloomsbury.

Billmeyer, R., & Barton, M. L. (2002). *Teaching reading in the content areas: If not me, then who?: Teacher's manual* (2nd ed.). Alexandria, VA: Association for Supervision and Curriculum Development.

Blachowicz, C. L. Z., & Fisher, P. (2000). Vocabulary instruction. In M. L. Kamil, P. B. Mosenthal, P. D. Pearson, & R. Barr (Eds.), *Handbook of reading research* (Vol. 3, pp. 503–524). Mahwah, NJ: Erlbaum.

Bloom, B. S., Engelhart, M. D., Furst, E. J., Hill, W. H., & Krathwohl, D. R. (1956). *Taxonomy of educational objectives: The classification of educational goals—Handbook I: Cognitive domain.* New York: David McKay.

Brand, M., & Brand, G. (2006). *Practical fluency: Classroom perspectives, grades K–6.* Portland, ME: Stenhouse.

Bromley, K. (2002). *Stretching students' vocabulary.* New York: Scholastic.

Bromley, K. (2004, May). *Rethinking vocabulary instruction: Best-practice strategies that work for struggling readers.* Presentation given at the conference of the International Reading Association, Reno, NV.

Bromley, K., DeVitis, L. I., & Modlo, M. (1999). *50 graphic organizers for reading, writing and more, grades 4–8.* New York: Scholastic.

Brozo, W. G., & Simpson, M. L. (2007). *Content literacy for today's adolescents: Honoring diversity and building competence* (5th ed.). Upper Saddle River, NJ: Prentice Hall.

Bulgren, J., Schumaker, J. B., & Deshler, D. D. (1988). Effectiveness of a concept teaching routine in enhancing the performance of LD students in secondary-level mainstream classes. *Learning Disability Quarterly, 11*(1), 3–17.

Buss, K., & Karnowski, L. (2002). *Reading and writing nonfiction genres.* Newark, DE: International Reading Association.

Cain, T. R. (2011). Thinking critically about undergraduate education. *Thought and Action.* Accessed at www.nea.org/home/50459.htm on January 18, 2016.

Caine, R. N. (2000). Building the bridge from research to classroom. *Educational Leadership, 58*(3), 59–61.

Caldwell, J. (1993). *Developing a text coding strategy for understanding expository text.* Milwaukee: Allyn & Bacon.

Calkins, L. M. (1994). *The art of teaching writing* (2nd ed.). Portsmouth, NH: Heinemann.

Campbell, B., & Fulton, L. (2003). *Science notebooks: Writing about inquiry.* Portsmouth, NH: Heinemann.

Carson, S. A. (1999). A veteran enters the reading wars: My journey. *The Reading Teacher, 53*(3), 212–224.

Casteel, J. D., & Stahl, R. J. (1973). *The social science observation record (SSOR): Theoretical construct and pilot studies.* Gainesville, FL: P. K. Yonge Laboratory School. (ERIC Document Reproduction Service No. ED101002)

Collins, N. (1996). *Motivating low performing adolescent readers.* Bloomington, IN: ERIC Clearinghouse on Reading, English, and Communication.

Cunningham, P. M., & Allington, R. L. (1999). *Classrooms that work: They can all read and write* (2nd ed.). New York: Longman.

Darch, C. B., Carnine, D. W., & Kame'enui, E. J. (1986). The role of graphic organizers and social structure in content area instruction. *Journal of Reading Behavior, 18*(4), 275–295.

Davey, B. (1983). Think-aloud: Modeling the cognitive processes of reading comprehension. *Journal of Reading, 27*(1), 44–47.

Davis, F. B. (1972). Psychometric research on comprehension in reading. *Reading Research Quarterly, 7*(4), 628–678.

Doran, G. T. (1981). There's a S.M.A.R.T. way to write management's goals and objectives. *Management Review, 70*(11), 35–36.

Downs, R. (2015, October 28). *Project based learning with students with disabilities* [Blog post]. Accessed at https://bie.org/blog/project_based_learning_with_students_with_disabilities on January 18, 2016.

Duke, N. K. (2004). The case for informational text. *Educational Leadership, 61*(6), 40–44.

Duke, N. K., & Bennett-Armistead, V. S. (2003). *Reading and writing informational text in the primary grades: Research-based practices.* New York: Scholastic.

Duke, N. K., & Pressley, M. (2005). How can I help my struggling readers? *Instructor, 115*(4), 23–25.

Ehri, L. C. (2003, March 17). *Systematic phonics instruction: Findings of the National Reading Panel.* Paper presented at the invitational seminar organized by the Standards and Effectiveness Unit, Department for Education and Skills, London.

Elkonin, D. (1971). The development of speech. In A. V. Zaporozhets & D. B. Elkonin (Eds.), *The psychology of preschool children* (pp. 111–185). Cambridge, MA: MIT Press.

Ellery, V., & Rosenboom, J. L. (2011). *Sustaining strategic readers: Techniques for supporting content literacy in grades 6–12.* Newark, DE: International Reading Association.

Farstrup, A. E., & Samuels, S. J. (Eds.). (2002). *What research has to say about reading instruction* (3rd ed.). Newark, DE: International Reading Association.

Fletcher, R. (1993). *What a writer needs*. Portsmouth, NH: Heinemann.

Fletcher, R. (2006). *Boy writers: Reclaiming their voices*. Portland, ME: Stenhouse.

Fletcher, R., & Portalupi, J. (1998). *Craft lessons: Teaching writing K–8*. Portland, ME: Stenhouse.

Freebody, P., & Anderson, R. C. (1983). Effects of vocabulary difficulty, text cohesion, and schema availability on reading comprehension. *Reading Research Quarterly, 18*(3), 277–294.

Fuchs, L. S., Fuchs, D., Hosp, M. K., & Jenkins, J. R. (2001). Oral reading fluency as an indicator of reading competence: A theoretical, empirical, and historical analysis. *Scientific Studies of Reading, 5*(3), 239–256.

Gajria, M., Jitendra, A. K., Sood, S., & Sacks, G. (2007). Improving comprehension of expository text in students with LD: A research synthesis. *Journal of Learning Disabilities, 40*(3), 210–225.

Gaskins, I. W., Ehri, L. C., Cress, C., O'Hara, C., & Donnelly, K. (1996). Procedures for word learning: Making discoveries about words. *The Reading Teacher, 50*(4), 312–327.

Gipe, J. P. (2005). *Multiple paths to literacy: Assessment and differentiated instruction for diverse learners, K–12* (6th ed.). Upper Saddle River, NJ: Pearson.

Gordon, W. J. J. (1961). *Synectics: The development of creative capacity*. New York: Harper & Row.

Graves, D. H. (1994). *A fresh look at writing*. Portsmouth, NH: Heinemann.

Gregory, G., & Chapman, C. (2013). *Differentiated instructional strategies: One size doesn't fit all* (3rd ed.). Thousand Oaks, CA: Corwin Press.

Gunning, T. G. (2001). *Building words: A resource manual for teaching word analysis and spelling strategies*. Boston: Allyn & Bacon.

Hall, L. A. (2005). Comprehending expository text: Promising strategies for struggling readers and students with reading disabilities. *Reading Research and Instruction, 44*(2), 75–95.

Hart, B., & Risley, T. R. (1995). *Meaningful differences in the everyday experience of young American children*. Baltimore: Brookes.

Hart, B., & Risley, T. R. (2003). The early catastrophe: The 30 million word gap by age 3. *American Educator, 27*(1), 4–9.

Horton, S. V., Lovitt, T. C., & Bergerud, D. (1990). The effectiveness of graphic organizers for three classifications of secondary students in content area classes. *Journal of Learning Disabilities, 23*(1), 12–22.

Idol, L., & Croll, V. J. (1987). Story-mapping training as a means of improving reading comprehension. *Learning Disability Quarterly, 10*(3), 214–229.

International Reading Association & National Council of Teachers of English. (2010). *Standards for the assessment of reading and writing* (Rev. ed.). Newark, DE: Authors.

Ivey, G., & Fisher, D. (2006). When thinking skills trump reading skills. *Educational Leadership, 64*(2), 16–21.

Jennings, J. H., Caldwell, J. S., & Lerner, J. W. (2006). *Reading problems: Assessment and teaching strategies* (5th ed.). Boston: Pearson.

Jensen, A. R. (1980). *Bias in mental testing.* New York: Free Press.

Jensen, E. (2005). *Teaching with the brain in mind* (2nd ed.). Alexandria, VA: Association for Supervision and Curriculum Development.

Jensen, E. (2008). *Brain-based learning: The new paradigm of teaching* (2nd ed.). Thousand Oaks, CA: Corwin Press.

Jitendra, A. K., Edwards, L. L., Sacks, G., & Jacobson, L. A. (2004). What research says about vocabulary instruction for students with learning disabilities. *Exceptional Children, 70*(3), 299–322.

Jongsma, K. (2001). Using CD-ROMs to support the development of literacy processes. *The Reading Teacher, 54*(6), 592–595.

Kagan, S. (1989). *Cooperative learning resources for teachers.* San Juan Capistrano, CA: Resources for Teachers.

Kelly, C., & Campbell, L. (2008). Helping struggling readers. *New Horizons for Learning.* Accessed at http://education.jhu.edu/PD/newhorizons/strategies/topics/literacy/articles/helping-struggling-readers on February 22, 2016.

Kendall, J., & Khuon, O. (2006). *Writing sense: Integrated reading and writing lessons for English language learners, K–8.* Portland, ME: Stenhouse.

Kita, J. (2011). *Repeated reading as a strategy to improve fluency: Practices for struggling readers in a first grade classroom* (Unpublished master's thesis). St. John Fisher College, Rochester, NY.

Klare, G. R. (1984). Readability. In P. D. Pearson (Ed.), *Handbook of reading research* (pp. 681–744). Mahuiah, NJ: Erlbaum.

Kos, R. (1991). Persistence of reading disabilities: The voices of four middle school students. *American Educational Research Journal, 28*(4), 875–895.

L'Allier, S. K., & Elish-Piper, L. (2007). "Walking the walk" with teacher education candidates: Strategies for promoting active engagement with assigned readings. *Journal of Adolescent and Adult Literacy, 50*(5), 338–353.

Lane, B. (1993). *After the end: Teaching and learning creative revision.* Portsmouth, NH: Heinemann.

Lane, B. (1999). *Reviser's toolbox.* Shoreham, VT: Discover Writing Press.

Learning First Alliance. (1998). Every child reading: An action plan of the Learning First Alliance. *American Educator, 22*(1–2), 52–63.

Learning First Alliance. (2000). *Every child reading: A professional development guide.* Baltimore: Author.

Lehr, F., Osborn, J., & Hiebert, E. H. (2004). *A focus on vocabulary: Research-based practices in early reading series.* Honolulu: Regional Education Laboratory at Pacific Resources for Education and Learning.

Lyon, G. R. (1999). *Why reading is not a natural process.* Accessed at www.reidlyon.com/ed policy/4-WHY-READING-IS-NOT-A-NATURAL-PROCESS.pdf on February 22, 2016.

Manzo, A. (1975). Guided reading procedure. *Journal of Reading, 18,* 287–291.

Manzo, U. C., Manzo, A. V., & Thomas, M. M. (2009). *Content area literacy: A framework for reading-based instruction* (5th ed.). Hoboken, NJ: Wiley.

Marcell, B. (2007). Traffic light reading: Fostering the independent usage of comprehension strategies with informational text. *The Reading Teacher, 60*(8), 778–781.

Marzano, R. J., Pickering, D. J., & Pollock, J. E. (2001). *Classroom instruction that works: Research-based strategies for increasing student achievement.* Alexandria, VA: Association for Supervision and Curriculum Development.

Mason, L. H., Meadan, H., Hedin, L., & Corso, L. (2006). Self-regulated strategy development instruction for expository text comprehension. *Teaching Exceptional Children, 38*(4), 47–52.

McCormick, S. (2007). *Instructing students who have literacy problems* (5th ed.). Upper Saddle River, NJ: Pearson.

Merkley, D. M., & Jefferies, D. (2000). Guidelines for implementing a graphic organizer. *The Reading Teacher, 54*(4), 350–357.

Meyen, E. L., Vergason, G. A., & Whelan, R. J. (1996). *Strategies for teaching exceptional children in inclusive settings.* Denver: Love.

Miller, G. A., & Gildea, P. M. (1987). How children learn words. *Scientific American, 257*(3), 94–99.

Moline, S. (1995). *I see what you mean: Children at work with visual information.* Portland, ME: Stenhouse.

Montelongo, J. A., & Hernandez, A. C. (2007). Reinforcing expository reading and writing skills: A more versatile sentence completion task. *The Reading Teacher, 60*(6), 538–546.

Morgan, B. (with Odom, D.). (2005). *Writing through the tween years: Supporting writers, grades 3–6.* Portland, ME: Stenhouse.

Morley J. (1991). Listening comprehension in second/foreign language instruction. In M. Celce-Murcia (Ed.), *Teaching English as a second or foreign language* (pp. 81–106). Boston: Heinle & Heinle.

Nagy, W. E. (1988). *Teaching vocabulary to improve reading comprehension.* Urbana, IL: National Council of Teachers of English.

National Reading Panel. (2000, February). *Teaching children to read: An evidence-based assessment of the scientific research literature on reading and its implications for reading instruction* (Reports of the Subgroups). Bethesda, MD: National Institute of Child Health and Human Development.

Neufeld, P. (2005). Comprehension instruction in content area classes. *The Reading Teacher, 59*(4), 302–312.

Nist, S. L., & Kirby, K. (1986). Teaching comprehension and study strategies through modeling and thinking aloud. *Reading Research and Instruction, 25*(4), 254–264.

Ogle, D. M. (1986). K-W-L: A teaching model that develops active reading of expository text. *The Reading Teacher, 39*(6), 564–570.

Palincsar, A. S., & Brown, A. L. (1984). Reciprocal teaching of comprehension: Fostering and comprehension-monitoring activities. *Cognition and Instruction, 1*(2), 117–175.

Pearson, P. D. (2003). Foreword. In N. K. Duke & V. S. Bennett-Armistead, *Reading and writing informational text in the primary grades: Research-based practices* (pp. 8–9). New York: Scholastic.

Pearson, P. D., & Fielding, L. (1983, March). *Instructional implications of listening comprehension research* (Reading Education Report No. 39). Cambridge, MA: Bolt, Beranek and Newman.

Pearson, P. D., Hiebert, E. H., & Kamil, M. L. (2007). Vocabulary assessment: What we know and what we need to learn. *Reading Research Quarterly, 42*(2), 282–296.

Pressley, M. (2000). What should comprehension instruction be the instruction of? In M. L. Kamil, P. B. Mosenthal, P. D. Pearson, & R. Barr (Eds.), *Handbook of reading research* (Vol. 3, pp. 545–560). Mahwah, NJ: Erlbaum.

Raphael, T. E., & Au, K. H. (2005). QAR: Enhancing comprehension and test taking across grades and content areas. *The Reading Teacher, 59*(3), 206–221.

Rayner, K., Foorman, B. R., Perfetti, C. A., Pesetsky, D., & Seidenberg, M. S. (2001). How psychological science informs the teaching of reading. *Psychological Science in the Public Interest, 2*(2), 31–74.

Resnick, L. B., & Hall, M. W. (2001). *The principles of learning: Study tools for educators* [CD-ROM, version 2.0]. Pittsburgh: University of Pittsburgh Learning Research and Development Center.

Richards, J. C., & Gipe, J. P. (1992). Activating background knowledge: Strategies for beginning and poor readers. *The Reading Teacher, 45*(6), 474–476.

Richardson, J. S., & Morgan, R. F. (2000). *Reading to learn in the content areas* (4th ed.). Belmont, CA: Wadsworth.

Robinson, F. P. (1970). *Effective study* (4th ed.). New York: Harper & Row.

Romano, T. (2000). *Blending genre, altering style: Writing multigenre papers.* Portsmouth, NH: Boynton/Cook.

Roskos, K. A., Christie, J. F., & Richgels, D. J. (2003). The essentials of early literacy instruction. *Young Children, 58*(2), 52–60.

Rowe, M. B. (1986). Wait times: Slowing down may be a way of speeding up. *Journal of Teacher Education, 37*(1), 43–50.

Salembier, G. B. (1999). Scan and run: A reading comprehension strategy that works. *Journal of Adolescent and Adult Literacy, 42*(5), 386–394.

Santa, C. M., Havens, L. T., & Valdes, B. J. (2004). *Project CRISS: Creating independence through student-owned strategies* (3rd ed.). Dubuque, IA: Kendall/Hunt.

Slegers, B. (1996). *A review of the research and literature on emergent literacy.* Urbana-Champaign, IL: ERIC Clearinghouse on Elementary and Early Childhood Education. (ERIC Document Reproduction Service No. ED397959)

Snow, C. E., Burns, M. S., & Griffin, P. (Eds.). (1998). *Preventing reading difficulties in young children.* Washington, DC: National Academies Press.

Southall, M. (2007). *Reading fluency and comprehension intervention for students with specific learning disabilities: Proven strategies for implementing reading intervention in special education, resource and inclusive classrooms.* Bellevue, WA: Bureau of Education and Research. Accessed at www.ber.org/onsite/course.cfm?CR=XRS on February 22, 2016.

Spandel, V. (2005). *Creating writers: Through 6-trait writing assessment and instruction* (4th ed.). Boston: Pearson.

Stahl, R. J. (1990). *Using "think-time" behaviors to promote students' information processing, learning, and on-task participation: An instructional module.* Tempe, AZ: Arizona State University.

Stahl, S. A., & Fairbanks, M. M. (1986). The effects of vocabulary instruction: A model-based meta-analysis. *Review of Educational Research, 56*(1), 72–110.

Strickland, D. S., Ganske, K., & Monroe, J. K. (2002). *Supporting struggling readers and writers: Strategies for classroom intervention, 3–6.* Portland, ME: Stenhouse.

Thelen, J. N. (1986). Vocabulary instruction and meaningful learning. *Journal of Reading, 29*(7), 603–609.

Tobin, K. G. (1987). The role of wait time in higher cognitive level learning. *Review of Educational Research, 57*(1), 69–95.

Tobin, K. G., & Capie, W. (1982). Relationships between classroom process variables and middle-school science achievement. *Journal of Educational Psychology, 74*(3), 441–454.

Tomlinson, C. A. (2001). *How to differentiate instruction in mixed-ability classrooms* (2nd ed.). Alexandria, VA: Association for Supervision and Curriculum Development.

Tomlinson, C. A. (2014). *The differentiated classroom: Responding to the needs of all learners* (2nd ed.). Alexandria, VA: Association for Supervision and Curriculum Development.

Torgeson, J. K. (1998). Catch them before they fall: Identification and assessment to prevent reading failure in young children. *American Educator, 22*(1–2), 32–39.

Tovani, C. (2011). *So what do they really know?: Assessment that informs teaching and learning.* Portland, ME: Stenhouse.

Twining, W. (Ed.). (1991). *Issues of self-determination.* Aberdeen, Scotland: Aberdeen University Press.

Uhry, J. K. (2005). Phonological awareness and reading: Theory, research, and instructional activities. In J. R. Birsh (Ed.), *Multisensory teaching of basic language skills* (2nd ed., pp. 83–111). Baltimore: Brookes.

Urquhart, V., & McIver, M. (2005). *Teaching writing in the content areas.* Alexandria, VA: Association for Supervision and Curriculum Development.

Vogt, M. E. (2000). Content learning for students needing modifications: An issue of access. In M. McLaughlin & M. E. Vogt (Eds.), *Creativity and innovation in content area teaching: A resource for intermediate, middle, and high school teachers*. Norwood, MA: Christopher-Gordon.

Wade, S. E. (1990). Using think-alouds to assess comprehension. *The Reading Teacher, 43*(7), 442–451.

Watts, S. M. (1995). Vocabulary instruction during reading lessons in six classrooms. *Journal of Reading Behavior, 27*(3), 399–424.

Weiner, B. (1979). A theory of motivation for some classroom experiences. *Journal of Educational Psychology, 71*(1), 3–25.

Wells, J., & Reid, J. (2004). *Writing anchors: Explicit lessons that identify criteria, offer strategic support, and lead students to take ownership of their writing*. Markham, Ontario, Canada: Pembroke.

White, T. G., Graves, M. F., & Slater, W. H. (1990). Growth of reading vocabulary in diverse elementary schools: Decoding and word meaning. *Journal of Educational Psychology, 82*(2), 281–290.

White, T. G., Sowell, J., & Yanagihara, A. (1989). Teaching elementary students to use word-part clues. *The Reading Teacher, 42*(4), 302–308.

Wiederhold, C. W., & Kagan, S. (1998). *Cooperative learning and higher-level thinking: The Q-matrix*. San Clemente, CA: Kagan.

Wigfield, A. (2000). Facilitating children's reading motivation. In L. Baker, M. J. Dreher, & J. T. Guthrie (Eds.), *Engaging young readers: Promoting achievement and motivation* (pp. 140–158). New York: Guilford Press.

Wiliam, D. (2011). *Embedded formative assessment*. Bloomington, IN: Solution Tree Press.

Willerman, M., & MacHarg, R. A. (1991). The concept map as an advance organizer. *Journal of Research in Science Teaching, 28*(8), 705–712.

Wilson, R. M. (1981). *Diagnostic and remedial reading for classroom and clinic* (4th ed.). Columbus, OH: C. E. Merrill.

Wolfe, P. (2001). *Brain matters: Translating research into classroom practice*. Alexandria, VA: Association for Supervision and Curriculum Development.

Worsham, S. (2001). *Essential ingredients: Recipes for teaching writing*. Alexandria, VA: Association for Supervision and Curriculum Development.

Yoncheva, Y. N., Wise, J., & McCandliss, B. (2015). Hemispheric specialization for visual words is shaped by attention to sublexical units during initial learning. *Brain and Language, 145–146*, 23–33.

Index

40 Reading Intervention Strategies for K–6 Students
Elaine K. McEwan-Adkins
This well-rounded collection of reading intervention strategies, teacher-friendly lesson plans, and adaptable miniroutines will support and inform your RTI efforts. Many of the strategies motivate all students as well as scaffold struggling readers. Increase effectiveness by using the interventions across grade-level teams or schoolwide.
BKF270

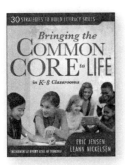

Bringing the Common Core to Life in K–8 Classrooms
Eric Jensen and LeAnn Nickelsen
Discover strategies to promote student mastery of the Common Core State Standards for English language arts across the curriculum. Develop the know-how to activate students' background knowledge to prepare them for learning and effectively structure teaching to empower all students.
BKF442

From Tired to Inspired
Mary Kim Schreck
In this Common Core State Standards–aligned book, educators will discover research-based tips and strategies to improve literacy from upper elementary to secondary school classrooms. Topics include teaching close reading and writing, engaging students, making literacy instruction meaningful, and more.
BKF594

Teaching Students to Read Like Detectives
Douglas Fisher, Nancy Frey, and Diane Lapp
Prompt students to become the sophisticated readers, writers, and thinkers they need to be to achieve higher learning. Explore the important relationship among text, learner, and learning, and gain an array of methods to establish critical literacy in a discussion-based and reflective classroom.
BKF499

Solution Tree | Press
a division of

Solution Tree

Visit SolutionTree.com or call 800.733.6786 to order.

Wait! Your professional development journey doesn't have to end with the last pages of this book.

We realize improving student learning doesn't happen overnight. And your school or district shouldn't be left to puzzle out all the details of this process alone.

No matter where you are on the journey, we're committed to helping you get to the next stage.

Take advantage of everything from **custom workshops** to **keynote presentations** and **interactive web and video conferencing**. We can even help you develop an action plan tailored to fit your specific needs.

Let's get the conversation started.

Call 888.763.9045 today.

SolutionTree.com